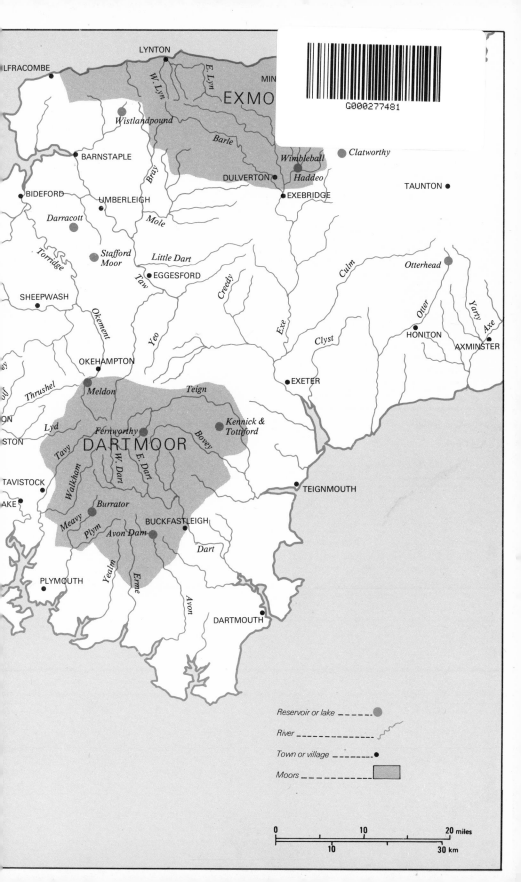

West Country Fly Fishing

AN ANTHOLOGY EDITED BY
ANNE VOSS BARK

B. T. BATSFORD LTD · *LONDON*

ISBN 0 7134 1883 4

Text set in 11/13 pt Linotron 202 Garamond, printed and bound
in Great Britain at The Bath Press, Avon

for the publishers
B. T. Batsford Ltd, 4 Fitzhardinge Street, London W1H 0AH

CONTENTS

✻

Preface   *page*   v

Acknowledgements   vi

Publisher's Note   viii

The Contributors   ix

Western Approaches *Brian Clarke*   1

The Land that Missed the Ice Age *Roger Hamilton*   7

Frontier Rivers *Conrad Voss Bark*   13

Taw and Torridge *Ted Hughes*   25

Salmon of the Moors *Charles Bingham*   42

Success with the Sea Trout *Roy Buckingham*   47

Trout of the Moors *Mike Weaver*   58

Trout of the Valleys *Dermot Wilson*   71

West of Weymouth *Wilson Stephens*   84

The Wet Fly *David Pilkington*   90

Bodmin Born *Marcus Ervine-Andrews*   101

Lake Fishing *Robin Lemon*   104

As Time Went By *Conrad Voss Bark*   113

Where to Fish   121

Bibliography   129

Index   130

With quotations from the works of Antony Bridges, Negley Farson, Viscount Grey of Fallodon, H. Plunket Green, Lord Home, T. C. Kingsmill Moore, Henry Williamson, and others.

PREFACE

❧

This book is about the rivers and lakes of the West Country, and is a distillation of the experience and knowledge of many people who have fished and loved them over the years.

It began as an idea to celebrate fifty years of fly fishing at the Arundell Arms, one of Devon's oldest fishing hotels, but as I thought about it the idea grew. No one, so I discovered, had ever written a comprehensive book about West Country fly fishing. I talked to others and this book is the result.

The rivers of the West Country are unique. There are over sixty of them in the three counties of Somerset, Devon and Cornwall, running down from the great uplands of Exmoor, Dartmoor and Bodmin, wild unspoilt rivers, what the French call *primitif*; and all of them hold an abundance of brown trout, and many have big runs of salmon and sea trout.

This is a part of England where kingfishers and buzzards still fly, where you can fish all day and see no one, where the rivers are bright and full of life and sparkle. So this book, as well as being about fishing, is a tribute to a heritage.

ANNE VOSS BARK   Lifton, Devon, 1983.

ACKNOWLEDGEMENTS

*

This book has only been made possible through the enormous help, talent, and generosity of many people. I would like especially to thank:

First and foremost our contributors, whom I am privileged to count as my friends, without whom this book could never have been written; our sponsors, Messrs Bovril, Matthew Gloag, St. Regis and Wiggins Teape, whose generosity made it possible to produce a book of this quality; our friend and photographer, Peter Keen, for his illimitable patience, enthusiasm and skill; the following for their invaluable help and advice and information: Herbie Symons, Horace Adams and John Ruscoe; Gordon Bielby, Dr Roger Merry, Stuart Bray and Clem Davies of the South West Water Authority; river wardens A. Mills and Mike Manning; Ernest Wright of Bristol Waterworks; the secretaries of many fishing associations and clubs in the three counties; Fred Buller, Hugh Falkus and Michael Beecham; the secretary and the librarian of the Flyfishers' Club; Daniel Farson for permission to reprint the wonderful description by his father Negley Farson of fishing the Barle; Miles Kingsmill Moore for permission to reprint the magical description about night fishing for sea trout by his father; Sarah Foot, and Joan and Terry Doyle for the legend of Tamara, from both their books; Wilson Stephens and the *Salmon and Trout Magazine* for permission to reprint his delightful article 'West of Weymouth'; the estate of the late Henry Williamson and Faber and Faber Ltd for permission to reprint the extract from *Salar the Salmon*; Lord Home and Collins Publishers for permission to publish the extract from *Border Rivers*; A. and C. Black for permission to quote from Antony Bridge's *Modern Salmon Fishing*; Janet Munns for typing the manuscript; and finally, my husband, Conrad, for his tireless help, encouragement and advice and the many happy hours we have spent fishing these rivers together.

Peter Keen, FRSA, who took all the colour photographs and most of the black and white, travelled the world for many Fleet Street papers, on special assignments to Russia, India and Africa, and in 1960 won the award of British Press Photographer of the Year. A former art editor of *The Observer*, he worked for *Picture Post* and the colour magazines of *The Sunday Times* and *Daily Telegraph*. He moved to Somerset from London in 1977 to be near his favourite fly-fishing rivers and now specialises in audio-visual production.

The other black and white photographs were taken by our contributors Mike Weaver and Dermot Wilson, and by John Tarlton, Ray Bishop, E. W. Tattersall and Charles Inniss.

AVB

PUBLISHER'S NOTE

✳

The Publishers wish to acknowledge the very real co-operation and support from the following organisations. Without their help, the publication of this book would not have been possible.

To the Arundell Arms Hotel at Lifton, Devon, as part of its celebration of fifty years of fishing and teaching on the Hotel's waters.

To Bovril Limited, which has a long connection with the West Country through its Ambrosia business based in Lifton, Devon. This was a happy choice of location by Ambrosia's founder— himself a keen fisher of West Country waters.

To Matthew Gloag and Sons Limited, Proprietors of The Famous Grouse Scotch Whisky.

To St. Regis Packing Limited of Launceston. St. Regis are based in Launceston, surrounded by some of the West Country's finest fishing waters. They employ locally more than 130 people.

To Wiggins Teape (UK) PLC. The paper used for the text of this publication was manufactured in Ivybridge, Devon, at the Stowford Mill of Wiggins Teape. For almost 200 years the Mill has been involved with the River Erme, first as a power source and now to supply process water. The ecology of this small river is of prime consideration to the Mill and, to ensure its purity, a fishery has been established in the effluent stream.

THE CONTRIBUTORS

*

CHARLES BINGHAM started fly fishing in Devon for trout in 1945 and has also fished the Dart for salmon for the past twenty-five years. For the past four years he has run a fishing school at Coryton, concentrating mainly on salmon fishing, when conditions are suitable.

ROY BUCKINGHAM, a true Cornishman, has worked on rivers all his life, first for eleven years as water bailiff for the Cornwall River Board; in 1969 he joined the Arundell Arms as river keeper and chief fishing instructor. He is a former Welsh Open fly casting champion and a member of the Association of Professional Game Angling Instructors.

BRIAN CLARKE is the author of the best-selling book, *The Pursuit of Stillwater Trout*, and, jointly with John Goddard, the equally successful *The Trout and the Fly*. As well as holding a senior job in industry he is also fishing editor of *The Sunday Times*.

LIEUT-COLONEL MARCUS ERVINE-ANDREWS, who was awarded the Victoria Cross at Dunkirk, started fly fishing as far back as 1916; as a soldier, he has served and fished all over the world. For the past twenty years he has lived in Cornwall where he fishes the Fowey and Camel; from 1977–82 he was secretary of Bodmin Anglers' Association.

ROGER HAMILTON, following a Cambridge degree in Natural Sciences, became a teacher; then for six years did research on salmon and trout in Scotland, before joining the South West Water Authority at Exeter as a fisheries biologist. He now has wider environmental responsibilities, including water quality and fisheries science.

TED HUGHES, D.Lit., OBE, Poet Laureate, is the author of many books which have won international awards and, in 1974, he received the Queen's Gold Medal for Poetry. He has fished in many latitudes between Alaska and New South Wales, but is more and more reluctant to leave Devon where he lives beside the Taw.

ROBIN LEMON probably knows more about lake and reservoir fishing in the West Country than anyone, for he was a senior official of the old Devon River Board and, later, the South West Water Authority; he also fished Chew and Grafham in their first years, and for many years fished the chalk streams of Hampshire and, when in the army, many rivers in Europe and Scandinavia.

DAVID PILKINGTON, our youngest contributor, caught his first trout with a fly tied by himself at the age of eleven, joined the Cornwall River Board as a trainee bailiff at the age of sixteen, and ten years later in 1976 joined the Arundell Arms as assistant river keeper and fishing instructor. He is a member of the Association of Professional Game Angling Instructors.

WILSON STEPHENS was editor of *The Field* from 1951–77 and for some years also edited the *Salmon and Trout Magazine*, partly concurrently. He has been a lifelong fly fisherman, strongly preferring rivers to still waters, and has a great reputation both as an editor and essayist.

CONRAD VOSS BARK, the first reporter to be seen broadcasting the news on television, was one of the BBC's correspondents in Parliament for twenty years; now retired, he lives in Devon, writes books, and is also fishing correspondent for *The Times*, where he worked before joining the BBC.

MIKE WEAVER, marketing manager for the West Country Tourist Board, has been a fly fisherman for nearly thirty years, is Devon correspondent for *Trout and Salmon* and fishing correspondent for *Devon Life*; he lives by the River Teign and is chairman of the Upper Teign Fishing Association.

DERMOT WILSON, MC, caught his first chalk stream trout on bread paste at the age of six; was a highly successful director of a London advertising agency before leaving for The Mill at Nether Wallop to start a high-quality fishing tackle mail-order business which he ran from 1968–81. He is the author of *Dry Fly Beginnings* and *Fishing the Dry Fly*.

West Country
Fly Fishing

BRIAN CLARKE

*

Western Approaches

It's NOT, as do all the others who contribute to these pages, that I know the West Country well; or even that I manage to get to it very often. It's the quality of experience that I've had on those big wide lakes, and soaked up in those intimate, pleated valleys that stir me to write these notes, that qualify me—if anything does qualify me—to appear in these pages at all.

What magic some of the names conjure up: Chew and Blagdon, Tamar and Exe, Taw and Torridge; and the little rivers—the Barle, the Lyd, the Carey; names that, over the years, have drawn me and others like me across those far-flung hills and along those winding, early-morning roads from London and Hampshire and further afield, on the promise of a few days' (or even a single day's) sport. Because the fact is, infrequent visitor though I am, that Somerset, Devon and Cornwall have given me some of the most vivid angling memories that I possess.

I've space, alas, to mention only three; and none of them, in angling terms, is of any great account. Except, that is, to me.

I remember an afternoon on Chew Valley Lake, many years ago. It was about three o'clock on a blazing August day and my companion and I sat listless in a boat, deep down in a bay; suffocated, burdened by the heat that bore down.

We fished monotonously, mechanically; each without hope, each locked away in his drowsing cocoon, hermetically sealed. We'd caught nothing, we knew we were going to catch nothing but still, after the journey we'd had, we couldn't bring ourselves to call it a day.

And then, a hundred yards away, there was a splash: just the one but enough, as any angler will understand, to break into our numbed reverie, bring our eyes around and zoom them in, like telephoto lenses, to burn into the spot where the ebbing rings oiled out.

A few moments later the surface rocked again and what seemed to be a thousand darts shot into the air. While they were still aloft a great trout slashed wildly at the surface and then, as our jaws fell open and our rods dropped lifeless to the gunwales, an entire shoal of trout hit the surface. In an instant we knew we were about to witness, though neither of us had ever seen it before, a pack of marauding fish attacking a shoal of fry. The violence of it, seen in ever more detail as the turmoil drew nearer, left us awed and gaping; Mother Nature red in tooth and gill.

Every ten seconds or so the water exploded into the air, as though Neptune's vast arm had thrown a cauldron of fry at the sun. Relentlessly the trout smashed in, now rending the water's surface, now bow-waving just beneath it; now concentrating the maelstrom of fry into a tighter group, for all the world like hunting dogs, before ramming themselves in again to cut out their prey; and now again, between attacks and roundings-up, lolloping head-first across the surface to pick up the maimed and the dead.

It went on for what seemed like an age. Before it was over the Roman circus has passed us by and was on its way out of sight. Around us, carnage lay everywhere. Trembling rings ebbed out from a thousand tiny fishes, gradually getting fainter with life itself.

Belly-up they lay, or spasmodically jerking along on their sides; some apparently regaining a lost consciousness, others instinctively, futilely, trying to swim, to put power into a tail that had become separated from the brain by a broken back.

It was like the aftermath of some great bomb, viewed distantly from space. So stunning was the spectacle, so awesome the result, that in all that time I don't think either of us threw a line.

The second incident which I've room to recount also occurred in Somerset, also on a lake; though this time I was alone, down in a bay, fishing from the bank. It was in the early days, before I knew even less than I do now about what might possibly be the cause of what.

And it was night. The sun had gone down to my left through an opal sky, the world had stopped breathing and the fish had come up. All of them. Every fish in the lake. In my bay.

In a lifetime one sees a very few such rises. This was my first. I think I know now what I didn't know then: that those seemingly numberless head-and-tailing trout were besotted by an immense migration of ascending and hatching midge pupae.

But whatever the cause of the attention, the fish seemed oblivious to everything else as they stitched slow, undulating, meandering lines across the still surface in front of me and slurped and wallowed and rolled. Certainly they were oblivious to my fly as, in fading light, I cast in ever-greater desperation—first at this ring and then that, gradually becoming more and more frustrated, altering the direction of the throw from one rise-form to another in mid-air, manufacturing a brand of aerialised spaghetti.

And then came the image that haunts me: the memory of a vast brown trout which adopted me, and that began to feed right down in front of me, beside my waders. I can't honestly say whether I saw it first or felt it—but so close did it happen that it could have been either: a movement in the water, close enough to touch. I looked down in time to see the great broad spade of a tail disappear from sight not a foot away. And then I saw it followed immediately by the head and shoulders as the trout began another porpoising roll, and then another and another moving in a circle around me not three feet away.

All across the bay other fish were rising, too. And as I fished on, ever more frenzied, it turned into a nightmare; like some awakening after death to a world of trout and then, after a brief moment's joy, having the elation crushed out by a tidal wave of awareness that one was in some fly-fisher's hell, doomed to be tormented and teased by feeding fish, close enough to lift from the water but destined never to succumb.

I pointed my rod to the sky and dribbled whatever confection I had on the point onto the water beside me, skating it around the head of my own fish, the trout that I could see but which was utterly oblivious to me. But to no avail. He simply went on rising beside me in a world that began with this fly and ended with the next, the gentle ripples he made lapping against my leg, rolling between my waders. He wasn't disdainful, he wasn't contemptuous, he wasn't anything. And I was neither relevance nor irrelevance: my fly, my frustration, my aching, my very *self* simply did not exist.

And then, after I suppose three or four minutes, he departed: he simply followed his tilting nose off into the nearby night, feeding uninterrupted all the while.

And was gone.

It was an experience that crushed me utterly, and which haunts me still.

I have another memory of the West Country. It is of the little river Lyd during the great drought of 1976. That was the year when, in most parts of Britain, no rain fell at all between April and October; and now, in July, that small stream, never anything of tidal proportions, wrinkled its way down the parched brown valley like a withered vein.

I was there to fish for sea trout. Miraculously, some had wriggled their way up where the water creaked its way through the stones in the shallows; and now, during the day, they lay in the few pools which remained, sheltered beneath the trees and the high over-hanging banks.

Sea trout fishing, as any sane man knows, is an evening and night-time pursuit and so, with the temperature in the eighties, I set off at three in the afternoon to try for one with the nymph.

A little way downstream from the bridge I found her. I'd crawled Hiawatha-style through the high vegetation and worked my way cautiously through the branches of an over-hanging tree, to look down from the cliff bank. And there she was, lying in front of a rock at the downstream edge of a long, deep pool where the bed sloped sharply up.

A few feet away the small, street-wise trout of the West Country, the urchins rather than the lords of the stream, drifted alertly from side to side, now darting forward to intercept something ahead, now waste-not-want-not sliding swiftly up and to one side to take the occasional surface fly.

But the sea trout did nothing. She simply lay there like a great grey shade; a submarine ghost against the pebbles of the bottom, motionless.

My word but she was big!

I watched her for a long time—perhaps half an hour, perhaps more; I've spent far longer than that watching undisturbed fish just being fish. And I came to know her intimately, as one always does; noticing, as one always does, that she wasn't really motionless at all. I noticed the slow twinkling fan of a tail that held her on station upstream of the rock, and how, imperceptibly, like a tethered kite, she responded to the tiny ribbons of turbulence which anxiously pushed past her, eager to reach the sea before the stream finally dried up.

But eventually, the hunter in me overcame the naturalist. I *had* to try to catch her. Cautiously I edged back along the bough I'd been lying on, crawled back from the bank to collect my rod, and moved downstream.

I had to go down a long way before I could negotiate the steep bank and get down into the water—maybe 40 yards, maybe more. And then, slowly, I began to pick my way back. I was immensely careful, lifting my feet out of the water like a heron, vertically enough to leave a hole in the water where my legs had been, to avoid that fatal push of water upstream and its rolling and chinking semaphore sneak. And whenever my feet went down it was to grope and read the bottom like shifting Braille, seeking stones that wouldn't move under my weight, crevices that wouldn't open up as the rocks moved aside, sending their muted thunder upstream to my quarry ahead. No man, I remember thinking, could have been more unobtrusive. Sombre clothing, matt-varnished rod, careful, gentle tread; I only just knew I was there myself.

Perhaps ten minutes those 25 yards took me, before I could see the rock and then the fish ahead of it.

Slowly I inched a yard or two more, brought the rod gingerly around from behind me and, looking at the fish all the while, groped up the cane with my left hand to unhitch the tiny, weighted fly.

One more yard, one more yard and it would be an easy throw. I dropped the nymph into the water to let the stream carry it behind me in preparation for the cast.

Now! Keeping the rod low I flicked it forward—and then an extraordinary thing happened. The fish, before that first forward movement of the line could straighten, began to dissolve before my eyes. One moment it was there, all distant composure; the next—the very instant I moved with evil but cautious intent—it began to disappear. Not with clouds of silt and rocking eddies, not with heaves at the surface and bow-waves behind. It simply dispersed, compactly; like someone walking off into a fog until you can't see him, can't see him, can't see him . . . any more.

And again, that's all. An event of consuming inconsequence. Simply a memory of a fish disappearing in a remarkable way when it shouldn't have been alarmed at all, shouldn't have known I was there at all. No dramatics, no heroics, no memorable struggle with *my* Moby Dick.

I've had those too, of course; at other times, on other days. But the memories of the West Country that I cherish most are made of subtler stuff: of images and atmospheres, incident and charm; and fishes and water and light.

Of the ether, as well as of the ethos, of the fly.

ROGER HAMILTON

The Land that Missed the Ice Age

WHEN YOU come to the south-west of England you cross a frontier. You step into a unique region of bleak granite moors and rich red farmland, a region with a multitude of tumbling rivers, narrow estuaries and high imposing sea cliffs. It is a landscape of enormous variety and a long history, stretching back for millions of years.

The peninsula is unique because it is the only part of highland Britain to have escaped the crushing effect of the last ice age and consequently the landscape is the product of an ancient geology weathered by other agents. Much of the region consists of sedimentary rocks. Earth movements elevated the land mass and then the long process of erosion began, with rivers playing their part in eroding and transporting the material.

As time went on the land was worn down almost flat and the rivers matured, developing meanders in broad flood plains. Further earth movements elevated the land yet again and the rivers, now rejuvenated, began to work afresh, cutting deep into the rock but maintaining their meandering paths. These steep-sided, narrow twisting valleys are a feature of the West Country. They are usually densely wooded and an excellent example is the Lyd Gorge on Dartmoor. Because the land mass has subsequently sunk a little, the lower reaches of many of these river valleys have been drowned and now the sea extends far inland along the estuaries. Areas of sandstone and carboniferous deposits were much crumpled by minor earth movements, the heat of which 'cooked' some of the rocks and muds into slates and shales. Other more disruptive movements forced molten magma to the surface, which on cooling became the granite masses of Dartmoor and Bodmin

Moor. Going westwards there are smaller and lower areas of granite, nowadays ending in the Scilly Isles. Perhaps the fabled land of Lyonnesse was a low area between two granite masses, now submerged and lost.

Rainfall is high, more than 70 inches a year on Bodmin Moor, 85 inches on Dartmoor and 75 inches on Exmoor but areas in what we call the rainshadow may have much less, no more than 30 inches or so a year. The rain is often heavy and localised and because of the impermeable nature of the ground it runs down from the hills very rapidly, causing water levels in streams that drain the moors to rise abruptly. A man may be standing knee-deep fishing one of these rivers and when a spate comes down water will rise over his waders in a matter of minutes. A very heavy spate we call a flash flood and occasionally these can be dangerous. The water colours, lifts, brings down a debris of fallen leaves and branches, and the flow becomes a torrent. Fortunately when the rain stops, a spate will go down almost as quickly as it rises. The quality of water in these rivers is generally very good. Dartmoor and Bodmin Moor produce a soft and slightly acid water while the streams draining Exmoor and east Devon have a little harder water which is neutral or slightly alkaline.

The rivers are small, very small indeed when compared with the Tay, Thames and Severn. In Devon the main game fishing rivers are the Torridge, Taw, Lyn, Dart, Teign, Exe and Axe; the Tamar which forms the Cornish boundary; and in Cornwall there are the Camel, Fowey and Lynher.

On the moors the river beds consist of good clear gravel, stones and boulders, but further downstream and in the east of the region there are deposits of sand and silt and the gravels may be compacted. A typical spate river has a sequence of shallow riffles and deeper pools. Even small pools may be several feet deep and are known to fishermen as guts or pockets where salmon and sea trout are inclined to rest on their journey upstream to spawn.

Rivers support an enormous variety of wild life, far more than people imagine, with subtle differences in the types of creatures in adjacent riffles and pools or even on the faces of a single rock. Where light penetrates, algae and diatoms carpet the river bed and form an important source of food. Mosses provide shelter and so do larger plants such as *Ranunculus* (Water Crowfoot). Rivers also act as a kind of sticky paper, collecting wind-blown debris, especially in the autumn. This is decomposed by bacteria and fungi, thus creating more food.

The list of river creatures is almost endless—worms and leeches, shrimps, snails and mites, stoneflies and mayflies, caddis, beetles, midges and gnats, the latter two being most abundant. The number of stoneflies in the West Country is a good indication of the high quality of the water. *Leuctra* (Willow and Needle Flies) and *Protonemura* (Early Browns) are common. Mayflies are even more abundant with *Baetis rhodani* (Large Dark Olive), *Ecdyonurus dispar* (August Dun), *Rhithrogera semicolorata* (Olive Upright) and *Ephemerella ignita* (Blue-winged Olive) being common. All these are of interest to the dry fly fisherman. There are many types of caddis fly, the most common being *Hydropsyche* (Grey Sedge) and *Brachycentrus subnubilis* (the Grannom).

Current, temperature, the substrate and water chemistry deter- mine the occurrence and distribution of animals and plants in the stream. Current brings food to many species, such as black gnat larvae and those caddis flies that spin a net to trap their food; but, for the majority, current is something to be avoided. Most creatures prefer to shelter in weed or under stones and in the gravel. The type of river bed is of great importance. For example the big burrowing mayfly nymph *Ephemera danica* needs just the right size of small gravel in which to live.

There are not all that many coarse fish in south-west rivers such as you find in the Midlands and the Fens. The grayling—which some call a coarse fish but which is closely related to salmon—is rare, occurring only in the Tamar and Exe systems. There are plenty of stoneloach, bullheads and minnows, which occupy the same areas as young salmon and trout, and they can be abundant. Here and there are plenty of dace and gudgeon, with some roach in the lower reaches of the Taw, Exe and Axe, and the Exe holds other kinds of coarse fish too. Eels occur pretty well everywhere, and the arrival of the elvers in early summer is a wonderful sight as millions of these tiny wriggling strips of life forge their way upstream. Eel pie is a famous West Country dish.

The most important runs of salmon in many south-western rivers are those of grilse and small summer fish, with small springers being much less numerous. Large springers are very rare and any fish over 30 lb is exceptional. Some of the more south- westerly rivers (the Camel, Fowey and Plym) have late runs of grilse, entering freshwater as late as December, and these are usually larger than normal summer grilse. It is often said that large rivers produce large fish and vice versa. Many theories have been advanced to explain why salmon return to freshwater after varying periods of time at sea, and evidence exists to support these different approaches. It would seem that there is a genetic influence, i.e. like breeding like, but there is also an environmental influence which may be overpoweringly dominant. Generally, small rivers tend to have summer and autumn runs of grilse and small salmon, whereas larger rivers also have runs of spring and larger fish. Superimposed on this pattern is one of long-term cycles of abundance of salmon of different sea age. Just now the proportion of grilse is increasing, at least in some of our rivers, whereas that of three-sea-winter fish is declining.

Sea trout are considerably more numerous than salmon in the south-west and they are present in most rivers, although relatively rare in the Exe. Their sea-going habit is extremely variable. Some trout never migrate and remain as brownies and others descend to the estuary for but a short time and are known as slob trout. Some go to sea but return within a few weeks in large shoals and are called school peal. Elsewhere in Britain these fish are known as whitling or finnock. The major runs of school peal are in July and August and the fish weigh around ¾–1 lb. Trout may spend a whole winter at sea before returning at weights around 2 lb and thereafter it is normal for them to migrate to and from the spawning grounds every year. Some reach a great age and size. A 10 lb sea trout may be eight or nine years old and have spawned five times. Older and larger trout enter the rivers at any time but the peak runs are in the spring.

Once these fish have been in the river for more than a few weeks they become very difficult to catch. Sea trout are capable of negotiating difficult stretches of water, normally impassable by salmon, and there are few places in the south-west which sea trout cannot reach. It is likely that many of the 8–10 inch fish considered by anglers to be brownies are the progeny of sea trout and would themselves have gone to sea in time.

All our rivers have been modified by man, sometimes to their benefit and at other times to their detriment. They are vitally important to thousands of different creatures living in, on, or near the water. We have talked about insects and fish but aquatic birds and mammals are equally dependent. The West Country has a fascinating community of birds, resident, passage and over-wintering, and still has a respectable population of otters. Rivers are vital to man too. See how most of our main towns and cities have developed at river mouths or on the flood plains close to the water. Rivers have helped to form the landscape and they control the distribution and life styles of a multitude of beings, including man. Since we are all so dependent on them it is in our interests to conserve them, to keep them clean, to respect them and to treat them kindly.

The Legend of the Tamar

The name Tamar is said to mean 'Great Water' but there is a touching legend which describes how the Tamar got its name. A nymph called Tamara longed to wander in the upper world and, although warned by her parents, paid no attention. On one excursion into the mortal domain she met two giants from Dartmoor, Tavy and Tawrage. She led them a pretty dance but they finally caught her, at which point her father arrived. He put a spell on Tavy and Tawrage to save his daughter and sent them to sleep while he tried to persuade her to return with him. When she refused, her father, overcome with rage, turned her into a river of great beauty and her would-be lovers into smaller water courses, the Tavy and the Taw.

LOCAL LEGEND

CONRAD VOSS BARK

✳

Frontier Rivers

THE TAMAR is the border between Devon and Cornwall, rising only a few miles from the north coast, near Bude, and going right across the peninsula to Plymouth in the south. For the Cornish it is a symbol as well as a physical frontier for there is hardly a river crossing where they have not fought against invaders, Saxons and Danes and English; and there are stories of fields by the river where unmarked dead are buried, where cattle will not graze because of the corpses underneath, where human bones and rusted weapons are still at times turned up by the plough; and some will point out to you marks on the walls of hump-backed stone bridges which they say were made by the hubs of cannon wheels from the Parliamentary Army as it crossed from Devon for the great assault on Launceston Castle.

It is the last thirty river-miles or so of the Tamar, south of Launceston to the tide at Gunnislake, that provide some of the best fly fishing for salmon that I know of anywhere in England, certainly some of the most exhilarating, and well worth travelling a good way to enjoy. It is not a large river, compared with the Tweed or the Wye, and the salmon are smaller, averaging 10 lb, with a 20-pounder rare, but the run is good from about May onwards, depending on the water. The lower reaches are best in the early part of the season in May and June and the upper reaches as far as Launceston best in September and the first two weeks of October. Most of this water is beautifully cared for, trees trimmed, croys built and ladders placed where these are needed.

The Tamar runs for most of the way through fertile agricultural land into which it has cut its way deeply, sunk down in many places like a Devon lane, so that as often as not when you approach the river all you see is a scarf of trees and you have to get within a few yards before you see the river running below. Grazing land and barley fields and thick woods line the banks and from time to time granite outcrops of the moor rise up to dizzying heights.

The river is coloured for most of the season, at least to some extent, though in low water it has a gently diluted whisky tint and is clear. A few heavy rainfalls in the upper reaches and the water rises and darkens with the run-off from the fields. Salmon are taken at all times but the best period seems to be after a spate when the river is falling and the salmon have just settled in the pools but are still bright and fresh. Then they will take a fly even in highly coloured water with the visibility no more than 18 inches to 2 feet. This is perhaps one reason why so many Tamar flies are fairly large and brightly coloured, so that they can be seen. Tamar salmon take a fly well, and many miles of the lower reaches are fly-only, but spinning is allowed, with some restrictions, in certain places; and further upstream, after about the first twenty-five river-miles, you will find the local farmers on their own water dipping the worm.

The character of the water changes considerably within a matter of yards, fast rapids, long shallows and deep pools follow each other with bewildering rapidity, making fishing fascinating and often difficult. Local knowledge, a fishing map, or a ghilly, are all a great help in finding where the salmon lie. Otherwise you may well fish a place that looks good but which seldom holds fish.

When I first came down to Devon from fishing in Scotland one thing that surprised me was the speed at which many of the local experienced fishermen fished the fly. They fished very fast indeed, and I was advised to do the same. One West Country fisherman, Kenneth Dawson, who wrote many articles and books about fishing in the twenties and thirties, was amused by the various opinions on fly speed; they varied, he wrote, from those who swore by the 'Ballyshannon waggle' which meant waggling the rod up and down the whole time the fly was in the water, to stripping the fly in fast, to not moving it at all. All have their devoted followers.

The advice of most of the experienced fishermen of the lower Tamar, the river keepers, the professional ghillies and instructors, is to keep the fly moving, though not all of them move it at the same speed. Horace Adams of Endsleigh and Roy Buckingham of the Arundell Arms water both fish at a speed greater than you would see on most Scottish rivers but the fastest stripper in the west must surely be Herbie Symons.

Now retired, and living in a cottage just above Gunnislake weir, Herbie Symons has known the Tamar for fifty years, first as bailiff for the Dukes of Bedford, later for the syndicate which now owns the water. He is all for fly fishing, very much against spinning, which he regards as unsporting.

I don't think there is any sport in it. I like to cast my fly, up to 40 yards if need be, and put it down, and then strip in and see the salmon dash for it. I like to use big single-hook flies. I've killed fish on 12/0 and quite a lot on 7/0 but I like best to use the 2/0 size because then I know the water is just right. The bigger ones you only use when the water is very fast and high and coloured.

I think the most effective pattern is the Yellow Torrish and next to that the Jock Scott. I use a 13 foot glass fibre rod with a sinking tip line so that I can strip the fly in fast and it doesn't break the surface. The speed of the strip depends on the direction you cast. If you're casting square you strip in faster than if you cast downstream.

I like to see all my fish come to the fly. The whole aim of my fishing is to bring the fly upstream and away from the fish so that the fish leaves his lie to dash after it. I suppose that nineteen out of every twenty salmon I catch I see the take. I see the salmon come up and close his mouth on the fly and at that moment I strike. If you leave it a second longer he feels the hook and spits it out.

Further upstream from Gunnislake, Horace Adams of Endsleigh will tell you that he always knows when someone comes down from Scotland because they cast the fly across and down, follow it around with the rod tip, and put their left hand behind their back. 'I always tell them—keep it moving!' He moves the fly fast but not as fast as Herbie though his tackle is similar, a double-handed glass or graphite carbon rod of about 12 feet 6 inches and a sink-tip weight-10 line. He says:

As for the flies, they are now totally different to what they were when I was brought up in the 1930s. Then it was a bright fly for a bright day and you put on a Silver Doctor or a Silver Grey in sizes from 5/0 down to about a 6. My favourite was the Dusty Miller. On a dull day it might be a Thunder and Lightening. In a cold evening you might go for a Jock Scott. The Yellow Torrish, which is now so popular, didn't come in down here until the late 1950s. But all these beautiful patterns on single hooks are dying out. Tubes are taking their place for they are so much easier to tie and I suppose something like 80 or 90 per cent of people who fish our waters are now using them. A lot of fish are taken on a purely black fly but I like to put a bit of colour into it myself, preferably yellow, especially in coloured water.

There are various patterns of the Yellow Torrish, some of them very complicated indeed, but the one that seems to be in use on the Tamar at the moment has a tag of silver tinsel with a golden pheasant crest, a butt of black ostrich herl, a body of silver tinsel with a bright yellow hackle, wings of turkey tail or brown mallard with strips of red and blue swan, a golden pheasant topping and a black head.

Even though many salmon fishermen are using tube flies, because they are comparatively cheap, easy to tie, and the treble can be replaced if a point goes, one wonders if there is not a slight movement back to the traditional fly, not the huge meat hook that Herbie Symons uses but a low-water single hook of fine steel and a fine point in the medium range of 2 to 6, or thereabouts. Fished with a sinking line they can go deep and they can always be fished close to the surface in the old greased-line fashion. They are light and thin and cast beautifully with no wind-drag at all and are ideal for a man who ties his own flies and is proud of them.

Fashions change. Much of this is a matter of personal taste. The meat hooks that Herbie Symons uses are bad hookers fished in a conventional way but not in his way. His fast stripping close to the surface is highly efficient.

My own box is full of tubes and singles and doubles and I seem to use all of them as the spirit moves me and as the conditions of the water seem to ask for them. There are also the long-shank trebles of the Esmond Drury type which are also very effective and good hookers, but I must confess that aesthetically—and one cannot ignore a sense of beauty—it gives me great pleasure to tie on a fully dressed low-water single with its bright wings and sparkling hackles.

Although the advice of all the experts is to move the fly fast on the Tamar, from time to time my inclination is to let the water do most of the work. A light fly in fast water does appear to have a life of its own as it flirts and flickers in the conflicting underwater currents, especially when the river is full of boulders and ridges which create myriad glides and flows and eddies at almost every level. You need, I think, a certain river craft to know when and where and how to move a fly, and when to let the water move it for you, and then of course there are times when a kingfisher or a heron will take your eye and the left hand forgets its cunning. All these things must be taken into account.

Most fishermen like to work out for themselves their philosophy of the fly and there are many ways to fish it. There are many holes or guts on the Tamar which hold salmon very deep down, how deep it is often difficult to say, and Roy Buckingham, on the Arundell water, has a way of dealing with these. He will stand at the head of the gut, use a fast-sinking line, let the fly go deep on the dangle, and then force it to go deeper still by plunging the point of the rod itself into the water. A deep hole can be searched easily and the method is highly effective.

In clear low water when a salmon can be seen, one Tamar fisherman fishes for them as if he is fishing a nymph on a chalk stream. He uses a very small weighted black fly, not much bigger than your finger nail, casts it well above the lie and lets it drift down over the fish. A pure Netheravon method! You need eyes like a hawk but in low water this often takes a fish when nothing else will do any good at all.

You have, therefore, a great deal of freedom to fish as you please, some one way and some another, and this is one of the delights of this river with its enormous variety of water; but another delight is in the country itself. When fishing a beat in most of this part of the world you are alone. You are in the wild. Parts of it are sheer wilderness. You hardly see another human all day. Maybe the man on the beat next to you will greet you on the bank at lunch, maybe you will see the bailiff, but that is about all. In the woods, you may hear a forester at work; but foresters, like badgers, are rarely seen.

One of the many lonely pools I love is in the heart of the woods. A stony unmade track skirts the sides of a thick forest of mixed pines and ash and oak. It is on the side of a slope and cut into it, and the slope is so steep you think the path is liable to slip away from it at any moment, and you go down this path, very carefully, ankle deep in pine needles and dead leaves, through columned trees and slanting shafts of sunlight. Here and there, steps have been cut and stones laid for you, for otherwise you could hardly manage to get down except by sliding. Suddenly you come out from the woods, with its shafts of sunlight slanting through the trees, into a dazzling blaze of sun and a roar of rapids. Great boulders stand up in the white water like the ruins of old temples and the spray goes over them in thunder and mist. You fish above and below these rapids from old stone croys; and it was well below, but still in very fast water, that I caught my first big Tamar salmon.

I had been casting idly, no doubt not as I should, because I was watching a pair of buzzards overhead, maybe five hundred or a thousand feet up in the sky, soaring on the drift. There is something fascinating about watching buzzards at that height with their outstretched wings, hardly seeming to fly at all, just drifting about the sky on thermals of air, mewing to each other from time to time. The sound of a buzzard is strangely like a cat's mewing. Do they talk? Are they exchanging signals? I do not know but the West Country is full of these lovely birds. As I say, I was absorbed in the contemplation of buzzards.

I was fishing in an idle kind of way. Here, with the woods so close and the river narrow and fast, making great turmoils of water, you need only a roll cast and you are a good half way across. I rolled the fly over, still half of me with the buzzards, and it fell in the curl of water just to the side of the main flow. It had hardly been there for a few seconds and the little tube with its red and yellow hackle seemed to snag. The river there is full of underwater boulders with a cover of weed and I thought it must be another of them. Then the snag moved.

Five times that fish went downstream, possibly six or seven, for I lost count. He burnt my fingers with the friction of the line on his first fast run in heavy water, and five or six or seven times I brought him back again, pumping him up inch by inch, for I could not move below him at all; and when at last he came to the net I do not know which of us was more exhausted. I had my flask with me and I needed it. He weighed 16 lb and it had taken me just on fifty minutes. That will give you some idea of the strength of the river and of the fish. The sea lice were still on him and he was perhaps ten miles or so above the tide.

I learned a lesson from that fish, as you do from almost every fish. That fly had flickered in the curl. I was hardly moving my hand. The fly obviously had had enough life and movement in the water to attract a take. Indolence, you might say, does sometimes work.

It is best, however, not to ignore the advice of those who really know this river. There is something to be said for the idle moment, for the observation of birds and beasts and river creatures, of hills and trees and light and shade which take your eye and set your mood. If you can combine such things with an occasional intentness on what you are trying to do with your fly you may well have the best of both worlds. At times you will be sure that a take is coming, and it does not, and at other times it will come when you least have it in mind. The late Howard Marshall, an admirable man, once wrote that he would not have fishing overlaid with science. I would not have it overlaid with too much effort either. If at moments you can stand and stare it will help make your day. Concentration on fishing must surely be tempered with a little indolence.

There is another frontier river in the West Country, one that for a large part of its way marks the boundary between Devon and Somerset, and that is the Exe. It rises as a clear-water brook on Exmoor, not far from Simonsbath, which is not all that far from the Bristol Channel, and if it were not for the tilt of the moor it might well have run a few bare miles into the sea at Lynmouth or Porlock or thereabouts, but it so happens that the land tilts south and the Exe runs about seventy river-miles or so through Tiverton to Exeter, through the town, and into the English Channel at Exmouth.

Now the Exe is a clear-water stream, in the upper reaches as clear as any chalk stream I know, and the best of the river, to me at any rate, you can see as you take the road north from Tiverton towards Dulverton. Park your car and look down through the trees by the side of the road and there it is, shining bright silver in the sun, shallow and fast, running over stickles, a river so bright and cheerful-looking it seems to demand to be fished.

The salmon run up the Exe fast, when the water is right, as fast as any river I know, and a few will be as high up as Exebridge in

March or April, and will take a fly in the coldest and shallowest of water, but you must use the most delicate of tackle and small flies. Nothing heavy. Big tubes are out of place. Above Exebridge, with its white-washed pub and medieval packhorse bridge, there are two lovely pools, as clear as daylight. You can see a pin on the gravel two or three feet down.

When you wade this water in sunlight it seems as though you are standing on a marbled pavement of gravel with flashes of light around your thighs from the reflections of the sun. A sunk line looks like a cable. Often you can see the salmon on their lies halfway across the river. Even when you do not see them, for they have a great habit of camouflaging themselves as weed or rocks, you may suddenly see a ghostly shape rising slowly to your fly. This is the rare moment when the heart and breathing stop. You have to wait for the take and you have to wait for another agonising second or so for the salmon to turn down with the fly before you set the hook.

The Exe, for a number of years, has been a sad river, There has been a great deal of disease—dead and dying salmon covered with patches of fungus have been a tragic sight. By 1979 however there were fewer diseased fish and by 1980 there was a noticeable improvement. In 1981 it was better still. There is at least hope now, from these indications, that the disease may well be dying out.

A Tamar fisherman going to the Exe has to adjust himself to the clarity of the water. Everything must be light and delicate and fine and one of the favourite flies is a tiny black fly, with a silver body, a Waddington tube of about an inch long with a 16 treble. Imagine a hook as small as that taking a 10-pounder! This particular fly is tied by Lance Nicholson of Dulverton, intended originally for sea trout of the Border Esk and the Rheidol, named the Loxey after Colonel 'Rags' Locke, in honour of his record with it for the sea trout, but now adopted for the Exe salmon as well. It is certainly the smallest salmon fly I have ever seen. You can use other flies, of course, but in this water anything big does seem out of place. John Ruscoe, the keeper on the Carnarvon Arms water, gives this advice:

I like to use a single-handed rod, for the river at Exebridge is not wide, not more than ten to 15 yards across, but it is very clear, so I

use a floating line with a sink tip and a long fine leader with a point
of no more than 10 lb breaking strain. I use a small fly, a Loxey, or
a Stoat's Tail tube or double, but with no more at the most than a
size 10 or 12 for low water.

The Stoat's Tail is a grand fly in this kind of river for even a wisp
of black hair with a little underlying silver to it can be seen for
miles, or so you imagine, and certainly any salmon in any lie that I
know will come up to it if the fish is in the mood. Mind you, I
would fancy something like a Blue Charm or a Hairy Mary on a
low water hook, perhaps an 8 would do but a 10 might be better,
for I like their colour, but this might well be kept in reserve after
the Stoat's Tail had been well tried.

I do not fish as fast on the Exe as I might on the Tamar. For
some reason or other it never occurs to me. I cast across to the
opposite bank and let the fly swing around, and retrieve, and take a
step or so and cast again. I do use my left hand but with only a
little pull, a figure-of-eight wind-in, now and again, just keeping
the fly coming in a little, but no more. I like looking around as well
as concentrating on the water. There is so much to see.

As a schoolboy I knew this part of the world well and Somerset,
especially around Exmoor, has its own particular fascination. I
love its crumpled hills and their strange shapes. Some are round
and moulded like a woman's breasts, some bow and dip and flow
like green water and some stand up high and shapely in a way that
reminds you of a pixie's conical hat. Some of the hills are
submerged in woods. Some are bare with a cluster of trees on top.
Some are almost bare and cut with fields but here and there the
woods creep up their sides in a curving way, like furry caterpillars.
These hills, in all their profusion of shape and colour, emphasise
the beauty of the flat meadows with their grazing sheep, the
thatched cottages, the old stone bridges, the wandering river.

In all such things the fisherman finds delight, and in so much
more; the flash of a kingfisher, the hypnotic rhythm of the
movement of mare's tails in the water, the sight of hatching flies,
the brilliant dazzling decorations of wild iris and bluebells along
the banks, and suddenly, while he is absorbed in all this beauty,
what he thought was the slow waving of water weeds in the current
will become the steadying movement of a salmon's tail.

HERBIE'S TALE

For more than 400 years many miles of fishing on the lower Tamar belonged to the Dukes of Bedford, part.of the huge estate of the Abbey of Tavistock granted to the family after the Dissolution of the Monasteries. Herbert Symons was ghilly when a member of the Bedford family, Lord Hugh Russell, caught a 27½ lb salmon from the Tamar. This is Herbie's tale.

It was about forty years ago and was the biggest Tamar salmon I remember. I know exactly what he caught it on, a 1/0 Silver Grey. He was using a Hardy Palakona 16 foot split cane rod and a huge brass reel which had been made by Farlows in Queen Victoria's time. The cast was a 10 lb breaking strain. The reel belonged to a BBC wartime announcer, Lionel Marsden, who had it from his grandfather and I have now got it with me in my house as one of my prize treasures.

Well, I had Lord Hugh with me in a boat on a tidal stretch below Gunnislake which is now known as Impham Meadows, and I think if we had not had a boat the fish would have been lost. It went upstream and down, two hundred yards each way, three times. There was I paddling after it and Lord Hugh hanging on the rod. It was an exhausting business with that heavy reel and rod and every time I shouted to Lord Hugh to 'give him more stick' he would shout back to me 'I can't Herbie, I can't—my bloody back is breaking!'

It was a bad time we had to control that fish and there were people up at the weir above Lower Cottage watching us and cheering us on but finally when we got up to the weir for the third time the fish tired and Lord Hugh managed to bring him up to the surface. It was the first time we had a sight of him. I got the net under him and his head came over one side and his tail over the other but I gave the net a wiggle and he fell in. Thank God he did! It took us three hours.

The Good Old Days

Fly fishing for salmon is seldom pursued in these counties
[Devon and Cornwall] *for the fish meets with such
formidable enemies as soon as it quits the sea that
comparatively few ascend our rivers. The intent of the
proprietors of our fisheries appears to be the annihilation of
this prince of fishes. The most impracticable weirs are
constructed over which it is almost impossible for a fish to
leap; in the pools immediately below, the rapacious fisherman
casts his net every tide; whilst above, if perchance a fish does
succeed in evading the cunning of his netting foes, a host of
spearmen are on watch by night as well as by day to immolate
the persecuted wanderer. . . .
. . . and beside the perils that await the parents on their
journey from the sea, their young are also in imminent danger
on their route towards the sea. The millers take them in traps
by thousands and dispose of them by the gallon to neighbours;
indeed at times they are taken in such vast quantities that pigs
are regaled upon their delicate flesh.*

G. W. SOLTAU of Little Efford, Devon, 1847.

THE SALMON AND THE FLY

The greatness of salmon fishing as a sport is indisputable, and we admit its supremacy. Its attraction is to be found in the largeness of the fish, the size of the rivers, the strength of the stream, and its tremendous uncertainty . . . and the art of fly fishing for salmon bears no relation to any other form of angling with a fly.

EARL GREY OF FALLODON, *Fly Fishing*, 1899.

TED HUGHES

*

Taw & Torridge

THE TAW and the Torridge are the only two north-flowing rivers
of any size in Devon. Their catchment area, which is roughly
square in shape, includes the whole north-west third of the
county. It is full of oddities, with the Torridge rising only four
miles from the sea, just behind Hartland cliffs (and nearly going
down the Tamar, which rises only four miles to the west), and
the Okement, the Torridge's southernmost tributary, rising in that
strange Dartmoor nest of Devon's rivers—Cranmere Pool (which
also gives birth to the Tavy, the Dart, the Taw and almost the
Teign, all within half a mile of each other), while away to the east
the tributaries of the Taw take all the water from the west side of
the Exe, the Barle and the Lyn.

The region enclosed within this watershed is still felt, by its
inhabitants, to be something of an island. The Cornish border to
the west, Dartmoor to the south, Exmoor to the east, and across
the north that long wrecker's cliff coast, pierced by only the one
estuary, which is in turn all but blocked by the most dangerous bar
in the West Country—these are ancient frontiers, real barriers, and
they go deep in the feeling of the place. They isolate what Henry
Williamson called 'the country of the two rivers'—a territory so
special that south Devon cattle, for instance, are supposed to be
unable to survive in it. Beautiful corners, in typical Devon
style—bulging green hills over deep cleaves and coombes—are
here in plenty. But 'North Devon' is still a name for the nearest
thing we have in the West Country, and maybe in England, to
wilderness—with the most backward and secluded holes and
corners, the wildest recesses, the most difficult to penetrate. In the
sixties, during the DDT crisis, this was one of the last strongholds of

the peregrine falcon. Even porcupines have established a beach-head here, and though they are repeatedly stamped out, they continue to crop up. To a native of North Devon, Cornwall is a crowded holiday land, south and east Devon are a garden for the affluent and retired, and England itself is a crowded modern place somewhere away east beyond Bristol.

Perhaps that is why, in his map of Great Britain's major salmon rivers, Anthony Netboy leaves blank the catchment of the Tor-ridge and the Taw, though he draws in the Dart (without naming it), the Exe and the Tamar. Those southern rivers are certainly more visible. The richly settled valley of the Exe opens itself through Exeter. The Tamar hurries to one of the country's most famous ports and harbours. And the Dart glitters as a national jewel in an often-crowded national park. But the Torridge and the Taw creep away north through a land to which the modern world has come late, and still only with difficulty. Henry Williamson did very well, when he wanted to express his sense of the secretive, archaic spell of North Devon, to embody it in an otter of the two rivers. The otter census is a good index to the real wildness of a place. And you are now more likely to meet an otter on the Torridge or the Taw than anywhere else in England.

In fact, in spite of Netboy's omission, the Taw and the Torridge, taken together, have been regarded historically as the most important fishery in the county. They were judged so in 1080 (when their value was assessed at 25 shillings per annum), and nine hundred years later, in 1954, when systematic modern records began, they still proved themselves so, accounting for one-third of all the salmon landed in the South West Water Authority area. The actual recorded catch was about 5000 with two thousand of them falling to the rods, while the total figure for the whole SWWA area was just over 13,500.

What this figure really means can be seen better, perhaps, if we compare it with the total catch of a famous modern salmon fishery such as Iceland's. Surprisingly enough, these two rivers—the Taw only fifty miles long and the Torridge only thirty-five—were producing in the mid-fifties a catch, net and rods, one-twelfth that of the annual average of the whole of Iceland, with its eighty nursed and protected salmon rivers. When we consider the finan-cial obstacles to salmon conservation on these rivers of ours, we should remember, maybe, that international anglers will now pay between £150 and £400 *a day* to fish in the rivers of Iceland, of which only the top fifteen can compare with what the Taw and the Torridge rod catch alone were twenty-five years ago. Not that we'd ever care to exclude ourselves with such prices—but convenient flexibilities are concealed even within the Icelandic system.

To bring it even closer home, we can calculate that those 2000 rod-caught salmon of 1954 (it was an average annual figure around the mid-fifties) work out, very crudely, at about forty fish to the fishable mile, which must mean seventy or eighty fish for many pools. Yet local fishermen of long experience remember that the really great days, on both rivers, were the 1920s. Those who hope that the fate of these rivers still lies in human hands—helpful ones—must wonder whether even the 1920s showed the Taw and the Torridge at anything like their full potential.

As a sea trout fishery they have performed even better, with nearly unbelievable peak years. In 1967, for instance, which was the year the disease arrived, the total sea trout catch for the Taw and Torridge topped 10,000, with more than 5500 falling to the rods. This was over half the sea trout recorded for all the rivers in the authority area—though it was a peak sea trout year throughout the south-west.

Anglers who have fished these rivers for forty or fifty years will smile at these statistics. And there seems little doubt—the reporting of such valuable catches being the human business that it is—both salmon and sea trout figures are on the low side. It must be remembered, too, that until recently many local fishermen hardly considered the sea trout worth mentioning. The real sea trout total for those earlier days—based on the known catches of certain beats—has been guessed at ten times the reported number, which gives a rod-catch of twenty or thirty thousand sea trout, even in average to low years. This seems phenomenal, and is no doubt quite a bit too high. But the fish certainly can be there in very great numbers.

They are often very heavy specimens too. One wonders how many of the big sea trout of the Torridge and the Taw are mistaken for salmon. Most fishermen out after salmon will have their hopes pre-set for anything over 5 lb. I well remember the lengths I went to to persuade myself that the first sea trout I ever caught—a 2½ lb fish—was a salmon. (The first salmon I ever caught did weigh only

3 lb.) But with anything over 7 lb it is occasionally difficult to be sure, even after plenty of experience. The final argument might emerge only in eating the cooked fish. It is a local saying: a sea trout over 4½ lb is one you give away, and not necessarily to your best friend. Still, in the Taw and Torridge at least you can hold a justified hope that your 12 lb fish is the double figure sea trout you have been hunting all your life. At the moment of writing this, after four weeks of April low water, the nets in the estuary are taking sea trout up to 12 lb—more of the really big fellows than for some years.

The relationship between the two rivers, the Taw and Torridge, is persistently strong in every fisherman's mind. Fishing on the one, you are thinking about the fish in the other. Good news from the one lifts the hopes on the other. It is only a geological fluke that has kept the two apart. They almost manage to join, near Winkleigh—twenty miles from the sea. At that point the Torridge, having come about fifteen miles south-east for the meeting, suddenly thinks better of it and doubles back north. The pair then meander the next twenty miles, through their two magical valleys, tantalisingly parallel, without sharing a trickle, till the barrier of dunes at Braunton Burrows forces the Taw across into the arms of the Torridge, and they go out over the perilous Bideford bar together, in old North Devon style—after a long, reluctant courtship a shotgun wedding!

The fisherman soon learns, however, what their differences are. For its first half the Torridge has been described as a Tamar. Coming down through those wet, yellow boggy valleys south of Hartland, with poor bits of shillet here and there, and forestry wilderness, the backwoods of the backwoods, the Torridge acquires a stain it never loses. All this upper part, with its little twisting and burrowing tributaries, is scattered spawning ground at the mercy of the farmers and their ritualised winter poaching, though you would think much of it too overgrown even for the boys who come after the brown trout with their Kraft cheese. The upper limit of the salmon and sea trout fishing is around Sheepwash. Here the river curves into deep river meadows, cutting its characteristic primrose and daffodil-bordered trench through the river deposits of loamy sand and pebbles, winding later in the year through hanging jungles of shoulder-high pinky-purple Himalayan Balsam. These are the beautiful beats of the Half Moon Inn, which stretch, with breaks here and there, down to the junction pool of the Okement and beyond.

A different kind of water is brought in by the Okement, from Dartmoor. Quite often, the two rivers are flowing from completely different weathers—one high and coloured, the other low. Like the Taw, the Okement comes off the Moor very acid (a Ph only just above 4), and like all Cranmere Pool's streams, prolific trout water. Formerly, the trout fishing in the lower stretches could be hectic sport—better in those days than the main river. But the Okement, slatier-looking than the Taw, and with bare gorges, is cursed by metal deposits and a large, busy quarry under the moor edge, where it crosses the tilted strata that overlie the granite. After the 1976 drought summer a sudden spill-out of pollution from those sources killed virtually every trout down to the junction with the Torridge. Wherever these disasters occur, in such acid rivers, the trout take a long time to show any recovery—as long as six or seven years to get back to half a pound.

The Okement has just been given a new career, though, and a chance to redeem itself. Until 1981 no salmon or sea trout ever got past the weir at Monkokehampton, only two and a half miles up from the junction with the main river. A successful fish-pass now lets them through, and during this last winter, salmon ran right up to Meldon, under the moor—fifteen or more miles. Salmon were seen spawning actually within the town of Okehampton, probably for the first time in hundreds of years. For once, luck seems to have been with the Torridge, and this 1981-2 spawning run was described by experienced observers as the most astonishing they ever saw in their lives, with 'fish up every ditch'. Where all these fish came from might well mystify the angler who has prowled through the river pools these last few years. It may be that they were unusually big runs of the 'greenbacks'—that near-mythical race of winter salmon that shoot up the river in December, spawn immediately, and never see a net or a lure. Perhaps, as some have suggested, the Torridge (and the Taw) is developing a winter run, at the expense of the spring, summer and autumn runs. Whichever it may be, the interesting thing is that this winter run can evidently survive the perils of the sea—in particular the hugely developed ocean netting by large commercial fleets, and the massive drift netting along the salmon migration routes, which suggests that the dwindling spring, summer and autumn runs are meeting an enemy which the winter run does not meet, somewhere inside Bideford Bar.

Below the Okement junction, the Torridge enters its spectacular valley, where the hills close in. It winds through the beats celebrated in Lemon Gray's book *Torridge Fishery*, and slips into an almost hidden world. When you come over those high tops, in the green Devon evening light, with the small, round hills huddling close around, and let yourself down among the marvellous female curves of the coombes, into the cleave of that river, you know you are entering a very strange land, a paradise—the sort that survives in few places. There are unforgettable pools, shaded under oaks, swinging and coiling through overhanging woods, with wonderfully varied water. At one point on Group-Captain Norton Smith's stretch, below Beaford, the river loops two miles around and almost completes a circle—a novelty, and a relief too, for the regular Taw and Torridge day angler. The sun looking over your shoulder, the strong light throwing your shadow, and your rod and your line's shadow over the eyes of the fish, which probably have to rise into a full face glare for most of the day, is often a problem on these north-flowing streams. (One remembers the Irish superstition—not so easily shaken off once you've heard it—that even to have the *day-moon* behind you is fatal to sport.) It was in the hut pool on this water that a Mar Lodge produced a 34½ lb fish, which held the Torridge record for many years.

Below Torrington, the river comes into view of the main road, but this doesn't seem to bother the fish, and one of the most illustrious pools on the whole river lies directly beneath the road wall. What do these wild, nervous creatures—fresh from salt water—make of the perpetual thunder of Bideford's traffic over their heads? Yet they take freely, salmon and sea trout, the whole way down, so it might even help. This is the pool where Mr Martin wearied himself with landing salmon—eight in succession—then passed the rod to his bailiff who landed another three, all before lunch.

Though it lies so close to the Torridge, the Taw seems to run through very different country. The upper section—above Lapford—is a sweet-looking little river, at its best. Until recently it was a grand trout stream, with plenty of fish over the half pound, and pounders turning up often enough. Like the Torridge, it quickly acquires a tinge, but this colour comes from the famous belt of red land south of Lapford. A Taw flood can look like blood. At the beginning of this century, the main river above the junction of the Mole—which is only about twelve miles from the sea—was dismissed as 'muddy pools, full of dace', producing hardly twenty salmon a year, with no fish at all getting past the weir at Eggesford. In those days, nearly the whole run of fish went up the Mole. Nineteen out of twenty was the proportion given, but the numbers of salmon caught suggest it could easily have been many more than that.

Of all the streams of the two rivers, the Exmoor water of the Mole seems to be the one best liked by the fish, and this tributary probably still has an advantage—Ash Tree pool on the Fortescue Arms water is still one of the most productive pools on the Taw system—but the run up the main river is now comparatively strong. Tom Pierce, the well-known ex-proprietor of the Fortescue Arms at the junction of the Mole and the Taw, claimed that the salmon of the Mole and the salmon of the upper Taw were two distinct types. He would give interesting examples. Of a pair of fish caught on the same day, both absolutely fresh, and both exactly the same length, the Taw fish weighed 15 lb, and the Mole fish (he caught it himself) weighed 25. And that, according to him, illustrated the rule. The Mole, evidently, was once restocked with Scottish fish, and the deep, thick type still predominates. In the same way the Torridge was once stocked with a number of fish from the Tay, and some claim to be able to distinguish these from the native type. Though all salmon populations show a good deal of diversity in size or shape or growth among their individual members from the egg onwards, Tom Pierce was in a unique position to test his belief, identifying each fish as his guests brought it in.

A recent development, among Taw and Mole fish alike, has been a change in the spring run. It is too early to see whether this is more than a temporary aberration, but these fish now hurry through the lower river, hardly resting till they pause in the junction pool of the Mole, then press straight on up the Mole, and up the Taw to Eggesford. Last year a man fishing the Taw upper beats had thirty fish before April. A canny weather-sense in salmon may help to explain this fast early run, which has been noticeable on the Torridge as well. Since 1978 the annual rainfall in North Devon has been 20 per cent above the previous average, with

all the extra falling in late winter. This February-March high water
has been followed regularly by a May-April drought. This present
year, 1982, the pattern has been repeated: early long-holding
flood-water, with early, fast, far-travelling fish, followed by a
drought that has cracked the clay. One curious thing has been
remarked on, this year. As a rule, the spring run of the two rivers
is made up of two-sea-winter fish, between 8 and 12 lb. On the
Fox and Hounds beats at Eggesford over half the salmon taken this
March and April have been heavier than that, with one of 19½ lb,
and scale readings of all the fish caught there gave three-sea-
winters. Over on the Torridge a March fish—also a long-distance
runner, up among the Half Moon beats—touched 19 lb. On the
Mole, an angler played a fish for one and a half hours before he lost
it. A weight of 30 lb was estimated. The bulge of heavier salmon
that have been coming in recent years showed at the end of last
season (1981) with several around the twenty mark and one on the
Rising Sun water, at Umberleigh, of 27½ lb.

What is not sure at the moment is whether those early fish are in
fact a normal spring run moving more briskly than usual in order
to get as far as they can before the drought, or whether the spring
run really is coming earlier, as part of the drift towards a mainly
winter run. This year, in particular, the fish caught in March
seemed to be no more than the tail end of the large run that raced
up both rivers in February—becoming pretty well uncatchable by
the time fishing started.

Below the Mole junction, the Taw becomes somewhat larger
than the lower Torridge, with noble pools—many of them having
noble histories. That springtime border of daffodils, primroses and
aconites is the same as on the Torridge, and in August you can fish
into pools that are nothing but the pink-purple reflections of the
massed flowering balsam, as on the Torridge, but here everything
is subtly different. The river is less secretive, a touch less wild,
taking its curves through a more open, gentle-shouldered valley of
farms that seem richer, clinging to the remains of richer estates.
And something of the Dartmoor and Exmoor origins of the water
seems almost visible in the current, which looks somehow brighter
and flintier than the Torridge. Even in this the two rivers have
quite different temperaments. Some of the best of the lower Taw is
fishable from The Rising Sun at Umberleigh. Six miles of electrify-
ing pools, with the fish only hours from salt water.

In the years I have fished these two rivers I have never seen two local anglers fishing in quite the same way, unless they were spinning. When the new SWWA regulation was introduced two years ago, which limited spinning to March and April, the number of fishermen after April seemed to be halved. (Unfortunately it coincided with—maybe even helped to produce—a new intensity of sophisticated poaching, and any immediate results failed to show.) Early spinning in the upper parts of the rivers seems now to favour the Mepps. I don't know if it is a better attracter than a Devon minnow in these Devon waters, but it is certainly a better hooker. If you see a Devon being used, it is probably a yellow belly—which seems to have ousted the old coppery brown. Mepps induce a certain monotony of style: they can't be bounced on the bottom, they make their user nervous of fishing deep, and they can't easily be hung in the current. One angler of my acquaintance took thirty-seven salmon one year recently out of the Mole junction pool on a small Mepps, and every fish took in exactly the same place—which indicates what I mean by the monotony of technique, as well as the deadliness of the weapon. In the right place, they will take running fish, and at the right moment they can produce thrilling action fished just under the surface like a fly, though for this I prefer a small Toby. Closer to the sea, some anglers swear by the big Tobies, in the early water. Up at Eggesford on the other hand, they are said to be useless. They are certainly not useless at an equivalent point on the Torridge, where small bright Zebra Tobies seem to me one of the most attractive spinning baits of all. Some anglers seem to do just as well with a fly, even in high, coloured, very cold water.

Once that spring run of salmon has done its vanishing trick, and disappeared into the holes of the pools, sea trout become the great hope. Big ones are usually being reported from the first weeks, and this year a 6½-pounder was caught well up the Taw on the first day. Throughout April this run increases, generally good fish, upwards of 5 lb, and occasionally very much bigger. They seem to creep in on any level of water, but they definitely like a flood. High water in the late April, May or early June is worth fishing very hard—not only for the new salmon which will almost certainly appear if the flood holds on long enough (four or five days—which will need repeated rainfalls), but for the big sea trout. Sometimes a flood at this time produces a bonanza—filling the river with taking fish between three and five pounds. Almost every year it happens at least once. When it happens it is best to drop everything and live by the river, because very quickly these sea trout follow the salmon and seem to evaporate. During these waves, as long as the water is not too coloured, and for some time after, it is very much worth fishing at night.

Every angler seems to have his own medicine for sea trout, and his own methods. Watching some of the local experts can be an eye-opener. If there are any rules about techniques, the only one that has seemed to me pretty general for fishing in heads and tails of pools in these rivers is to fish the fly quite fast. There seem to be no rules at all about the type of fly. In his book *Torridge Fishery*—a good manual of techniques for the Torridge— Lemon Gray dismisses the Peter Ross. The most consistently successful sea trout angler I know uses nothing else, and rarely anything else but a size 10—and that on what was Lemon Gray's own water. The most successful fly I ever had was a worn out salmon fly, size 6—a bit of yellow hackle, and scrap of yellow wing overlaid with a couple of darkish strands, and a silver body. It would seem a simple lure to imitate, but since I lost it my imitations have caught only the odd fish.

The traditional local fly is Queen of the River—somewhat like a silver-bodied March Brown. The Butcher is a popular fly, and on the lower river I know at least two anglers who favour a Lady Caroline, which seems good for both sea trout and salmon. A roll-call of all the local anglers would probably produce quite a roll-call of favoured flies. In general I use a Silver Invicta, an Invicta, or a Stoat's Tail—silver-bodied or black-bodied according to my mood—in various sizes, or nymphs. When these fail, I start experimenting—but these usually seem to work for me, if anything will. I have noticed that a small fly, a tiny Stoat's Tail maybe, drifted deep in the deeper pools, and worked a little, will sometimes perform wonders, especially on a very, very fine nylon. It is usually good to assume that salmon and sea trout have magnifying lenses in their eyes (Frank Buckland thought he had proved they have: he took the lens out of a salmon's eye and looked through it). I have repeatedly noticed how much sea trout seem to like a Silver Doctor—even quite a big one—when it is fished fast, on a day of sunny clouds. Lemon Gray's favourite was a Mallard and Claret, and many anglers seem to agree with him.

He has a curious story of dressing one of these flies—almost by accident—with a few turns of yellow at the tail-end of the body, and discovering that he had invented *the* killing fly for that season on his water, for both sea trout and salmon. Experiments are often worth it. I had an odd experience a couple of years ago, fishing across the tail of the Weir Pool at Beam. It was a sunny cloudy day, eleven a.m., and in slightly coloured water I had a small peal, about ¾ lb, first cast on a small Silver Invicta. I released him, and fished across again for a while without moving anything else.

Some shoal fish (rainbow trout, for instance, and mackerel) seem to have extraordinary intercommunication systems, for relaying detailed information about dangerous objects (and pleasant objects too, no doubt), but it seems to take a little time to get through, so if you kill the rainbows you catch out of a shoal you can often go on catching them, but if you prick and lose one, or return one you've caught, the chances are the whole shoal loses interest in your fly. But the whole shoal will be interested in a new different fly. Where you can see the fish you can sometimes watch this happening. So on this day, I changed my fly to a silver-bodied Stoat's Tail, and straight away first cast had another little peal. I released this too, and went on fishing without a touch. I then changed the fly, and immediately caught another, which I released. I had eight silver-bodied flies of different kinds, and I caught eight fish, all the same size, all of which I released. At each first or second cast with a new fly, I caught a fish. After the eighth, I went back to my Silver Invicta, but that was it. I couldn't stir another one of them—nor with any other kind of fly. What I did not try was killing one of the fish and fishing on with the same fly. I have tried this trick again, but with never the same mechanical sort of success. More usually, the shoal ignores me after one lost fish. Or sometimes one takes again, next cast, same fly.

The first big wave of small school peal arrives in late June, and with a rise of water at that time they usually appear quite suddenly through all the beats. From this time on, the influx is as a rule fairly steady, helped by any spates, though not depending on them. Bigger fish continue to come in, scattered among the shoals. On the right kind of night, sport can be exciting from this time right up to the end of the season. But how rarely the night seems to be just right! Usually a promising dusk, which might yield a fish or two, suddenly cools under a clearing sky, mist blooms out of the pools and crawls across the river meadows. I have occasionally stayed, remembering Falkus' dictum that sea trout 'can be caught at any time'—or misremembering, perhaps—but I have never had anything to change my notion that these nights are made for bed. August is a better month here than July, the catch might be up a quarter or even a third, while September drops back to about the same. A good deal depends on knowing exactly where the fish are, and of course on the fish deciding to co-operate. But often enough, one gets it right. The most enthralling thing about Torridge and Taw sea trout night fishing is that the least touch can be anything from half a pound to seven or eight—which is like the difference between a swallow and a tiger. There is a weird kind of anticipatory terror about this, and it leaks an especially high-quality adrenalin into the blood—which is no doubt the drug we are hooked on. But it does need that possibility of a very big fish—which in the dark is a terrifyingly big fish. Much of the awe and mystery of the river at night comes from this hopeful sort of dread. It is something that I for one never quite feel on those Irish rivers at night, where the biggest fish will hardly be three pounds, and quite manageable.

Again and again the last week in September turns out to be one of the most interesting weeks. If there is high water at this time, and there often is, the whole population of the river seems to be on the move, and sometimes you pick up unexpectedly large browns, fish that were probably uncatchable in their own hide-outs, but now, moving up with the sea trout, growing excited and aggressive in unfamiliar new places. This is the week, too, that can bring the big salmon—the traditional weight for autumn fish is around 17 lb.

Fishing the summer run of sea trout in low water by day can be fascinating business. Here you see the real artists—with a dry fly, or a nymph in the deep holes, or a Tup's dangled across the shrunken spill of broken water in the neck of a pool. If there is a salmon in the pool, some old, potted, manic-depressive waiting for his evening crash-about, those last two methods are quite likely to connect with him.

No reliable run of summer salmon manages to enter the Torridge and the Taw. Strangely enough, quite a big run arrives in the estuary, brought in on the little flash-spates of July and August, but it takes an exceptional, prolonged flood to get any past the nets. If those two months are very dry, the proportion of rod-caught to net-caught salmon can make the rod-fishermen despair. It can be as high as seventy to one—seven hundred to ten, which must sometimes mean seven hundred fresh and recorded incoming fish to the nets, and ten old stirred-up red fish to the rods. When fish are running freely into the rivers, as in a wet April, the proportion is closer to one to one, and is some (at present unknown) fraction of the run. But quite often in those two summer months it appears that the whole run is killed.

There is no doubt that the Taw and the Torridge have entered a critical phase in their history as a fishery. The general plight of the Atlantic salmon, after about sixteen years of disease, heavy commercial fishing at sea, and increasing pollution everywhere, is deplored by everyone interested in this fish, but the Taw and the Torridge seem to be presenting the species with a peculiar problem. Between 1963 and 1979 the total sw catch remained fairly steady, but in the Taw and the Torridge there was a noticeable decline.

Before this induces too much gloom, we should remember that there is no radical change until there is a crisis, and that extreme ups and downs of fortune are no new thing on these two rivers. We have seen the high value put on the fishery in 1080, and a catch of 5000 salmon recorded in 1954 when modern records began. But between those two dates there passed a dark age of literally hundreds of years during which the Taw and the Torridge were not worth a cast.

The culprits here—as elsewhere—were the weirs. On the Torridge and its tributaries alone there were seventy-five of them, many of stone, and none with a fish-pass. When we complain of pollution, we should remind ourselves that we are struggling with a problem only forty years old, and only officially recognised as a problem worth solving for about ten. But the problem of the weirs lay there for centuries. How the run kept going at all is a miracle: presumably the long, high floods of those days before water abstraction and when farm-drainage was primitive and much of Devonshire still woodland and bog, enabled some fish to get through and spawn somewhere—enough to keep twenty-two boats netting the estuary all year around, and to justify fish traps in the lower weirs, and to supply a God-given harvest of smolts— which were thought to be a species of their own. Even so, the fish must have been few enough. It comes as a shock to learn that in 1861 and '62, when the opening of the weirs finally got under way, fresh salmon were caught on the Taw above Umberleigh (six miles from tidal water) and on the Torridge above Weare Giffard (at the head of tidal water) *for the first time in living memory.* When we have shaken our heads over this, it comes as another slight shock to realise that even after 120 years this dismantling of the unused weirs is only now being completed. The Eggesford weir was opened only a dozen or so years ago, the Monkokehampton weir only last year, and the weir at North Tawton—which witholds about one-seventh of the Taw from its salmon and sea trout—is still closed.

The positive way to look at this, of course, is to see that the swwa is at last doing what nobody up to now has been able to do, with the result that quite suddenly the two rivers have more spawning potential—in area of accessible gravel—than they have had since the Saxons started building their weirs in the sixth century. For the Torridge, the Monkokehampton fish-pass has opened the spawning ground of the Okement—reckoned about seven miles of suitable gravel. For the Taw, the fish-pass at Eggesford opened the spawning tributaries of the Dalch and the Yeo, and thirteen miles of main river (a quarter of the whole river), some of it the best spawning gravel in the West Country. And when the North Tawton weir is opened, as is planned, a further seven miles or so will be added to that.

Once the lower weirs began to open, the run seemed to recover remarkably quickly. But the nets kept pace, and pursued the fish up the rivers. By 1872 there were twenty-one nets in the Taw, thirty-three in the Mole, and three in the Bray. By the mid-1880s there were over fifty in the Torridge. The nets had replaced the weirs. Rod-fishing for sea trout, which had developed tremendously, almost petered out, and salmon fishing again became very poor. So it was only with the first real regulation of the nets, when their numbers were fixed at thirty-six, and the netting restricted to the estuary, early this century, that the modern history of the salmon and sea trout runs on the two rivers can be said to have begun.

What followed is astonishing in its way, and worth trying to analyse—even though big changes in the rivers themselves, over the last fifty years, put any certain conclusions beyond us. If we count five or six years as a salmon generation, we can see that what we now look back on as the golden years—the 1920s—were created by a mere four generation build-up of salmon. And since the nets came on in those days at the beginning of May, and from June onward took pretty well the whole summer run, as they still do, it seems clear that those boom years were produced almost exclusively by spring fish. But in 1922, when the opening date for the nets was brought forward to mid-April, and then again in 1928 when it was brought forward to 1 April, the days of that developing run of spring fish were numbered. Whether the nets alone were to blame, or the nets plus some new factor in the changing rivers—increasing pollution, the effects of water-abstraction—is a matter for debate. But it is a suggestive sequence of events. Among other things, it makes us realise that the true potential of these two rivers, as salmon farms and sport fisheries, has never been anything like fully developed within historical times. It also suggests that their natural potential, compared to most other rivers of similar size, must be quite unusually great.

Unfortunately, their uses in other directions, hostile to the fish, continue to win priority. It is a moot point whether salmon and trout in general, and these two rivers in particular, will ever draw any solid benefit from the very new and now rapidly expanding awareness of the need to control pollution at all levels, and to manage fish-stocks in a practical way, with international co-operation. But we have to hope. And that is why the effort to conserve the stocks in these two rivers through these next years deserves all the help fishermen can give it. And why the SWWA should be encouraged to keep up and even increase their protective legislation.

Spring Spate

Gradually the air was growing less cold in the valley. The wind eddied slower, warmer. Sunshine heated the opening buds of alders and for a while their lichened branches steamed slightly, with iridescence, then invisibly. A spider drew itself from shelter behind loose dead bark, walked into the sun rays, rested and warmed itself, moved as a branch shadow moved; and towards noon, with sudden elation, threw a gossamer into the air. Other gossamers were floating. They were signals of the air's buoyancy. Water was absorbing oxygen rapidly.

And all of a sudden, as though they had been awaiting a signal, all the salmon in the pool began to move, slowly at first, cruising just under the surface; then accelerating. One after another they leapt at the air. Far up and down the river, in the tails of pools and from the braided edges of the eddies, mile upon mile of grey swilling water broke with splashes.

HENRY WILLIAMSON, *Salar the Salmon* (Faber edn), 1972.

While up the Dart past Dittisham
The salmon swim from sea
To hang in the pools by Hexworthy
For the likes o' you and me.

ANTHONY BRIDGES, 1939.

The Dart claims a heart a year.

OLD PROVERB

CHARLES BINGHAM

*

Salmon of the Moors

LIKE MANY of the Irish and Scottish rivers that run down steep and fast into the sea from high granite hills, the rivers of southern Devon that rise on Dartmoor cannot give you consistent salmon fishing. Everything depends on the rain. After a spate you have to be there to make the best of the fishing that will follow, maybe for a couple of days, a day, even sometimes for a matter of hours. It is not the kind of salmon fishing that you find on the big rivers like the Exe and Tamar, but wild, needing rough walking, a taste for solitude, an indifference to rain and wind, and the stalking of individual fish in their lies.

The Teign, the Dart and the Tavy are early rivers, and the runs build up as February and March unfold. By April and May you can find fish as high up as the moors. About a quarter of the annual rod catch of salmon on the Dart will be taken in the Buckfastleigh area in February and March, which is about ten river-miles above the estuary. Pretty cold fishing too, if there is a north wind coming off the moor. These spring fish are often over 10 lb and I have caught them up to 18 lb.

Local knowledge is essential. Those who live by the river know when it is worth going for salmon, when a particular rock is covered or the water is between certain marks on a gauge. If you are at a distance from the river you have to rely on the weather forecast. In my own case, living fifteen miles away, I up-end the lid on my dustbin and if it is full of water in the morning it is worth the journey.

You will probably find that the first hour or two of the spate, just as the water level in the river starts to rise, can be good for a take, and that does happen, but the best water is when the spate drops away. It is then that you can fish all the likely lies. The water in these granite-born streams does not colour much except in the lower reaches; even in a flood there is just what we call a stain of colour in it, except after very dry conditions, so that when the water drops to low you have to hide yourself from the fish and creep and crawl; and then it is a good idea to work your fly in the rapid run-in at the head of a pool. If a fish is there, and in the mood, it can be very exciting. He lifts up, opens his mouth, and then drops back. You raise your rod as his jaws close and his head disappears.

In low water it is not all that difficult to pick out some of the lies, and even sometimes see the fish on them. Big boulders in these rivers are unmoved even in the heaviest of winter floods so that the salmon lies remain more or less the same for year after year.

In high water it is a good idea to fish the tail of the pools, where a fish may have just come in and is resting. Cast a big fly across to the far bank, mend the line, and let the fly swim over the tail. At some time or another will come that marvellous moment when a fish comes up in a long sweeping curve, showing its back as it takes the fly.

For tackle, I use a 25-year-old Hardy cane rod and I carry a Gye net in a sling on my back. A net is better than a tailer to land a fish. A tailer will not hold a slim grilse, because a grilse has no knuckle at the base of the tail to hold the wire, and a net is best to use if you want to return a kelt or, in autumn, a hen fish heavy with spawn, for it does no damage.

As for flies, at one time I used to use small Hairy Mary or Thunder and Lightning singles. They hooked well but because they had to be fished with fine nylon there were too many breakages, of either the hook or of the nylon, especially if the fish snagged itself around one of those big rocks which you get so frequently in these kind of rivers. So now I use tube flies with a nylon of no less than 17 lb breaking strain. This does sound rather like a 'killer's outfit' but to my mind it is quite inexcusable to lose a salmon on light tackle and condemn him to some months of river life with a hook in his mouth and maybe trailing a couple of yards of nylon behind him.

For floating line summer fishing the tube flies need be no more than an inch or 1½ inches. For early spring fishing with a sunk line you may need a two-incher. For the trebles I like no. 8 outpoint or for a 2 inch tube a no. 6. I find that the smaller trebles, the 10s and 12s, may not take sufficiently deep hold. For the dressing, I think the most effective colours are black and orange and a natural brown bucktail—one or two of those colours—and the tube body striped with silver or gold ribbing and long cheeks of jungle cock or jungle cock substitute.

One of my favourite tubes, a consistent catcher of salmon, and of big sea trout during the day too, is the Copper Dart. The heavy body is made of copper wire in close turns, jungle cock cheeks, and a thin orange bucktail dressing. The glint of copper under the orange fibres is very attractive, particularly in bright sunshine in the first stages of a spate. All tube flies should have sockets to hold the treble level with the body so that the hook does not hang down at an angle and get caught up with the nylon.

So far as the rest of the tackle is concerned, in these fast and rocky rivers with their rough banks you do need to travel light. Wear a waterproof watch, do not carry a camera or a wallet, for if the rain does not reach such things the river can, especially if you have to chase a salmon downstream from one pool to the next. You need little more than a few flies in a box, a spool of nylon, and a piece of binder twine to carry the fish back to the car.

On these rivers you are not fishing from man-made croys or from banks that have been specially prepared for fishermen such as you get on the bigger rivers. When you are 'backing-up' you will have to walk backwards over ground that is pretty uneven, to say the least. 'Backing-up' is useful in a high wind. You cast a small fly square across the river and then walk upstream, backwards, at the same time stripping in line as you go. This will often startle a torpid salmon into a violent rise that is so unexpected you feel you are going to have a heart attack. Honestly, to survive this kind of fishing you really do need to be fit.

Now about sea trout.

The Teign, Dart and Tavy are really very good sea trout rivers and in June, July and August the visiting angler may often stand a better chance with the sea trout than the salmon. Sea trout fishing in these rivers is no good in a spate—unlike the salmon—for you need quiet settled conditions for them to take best, and low water is no disadvantage. The best fishing on the Dart is near Buckfastleigh and if you don't know the river and there is no one to show you the pools the only thing to do is to go out during the day and explore, using Polaroid glasses and, if need be, climbing a tree so you can look directly down through the water. Doing this I've been able to count as many as eighty sea trout lying out in the pool with the sun shining down on them—a wonderful sight!

The best way of taking sea trout is at night, keeping in mind there are no such things as ghoulies and ghosties and long-legged beasties which materialise at night any more than they do during the day. There will be big fish in the pools by April and May, running through until August, when the smaller fish, between ½ to 2 lb, will predominate but because there is always the chance of a monster, never fish fine, never go below a point of about 9 lb breaking strain.

For tackle, I like to use ordinary reservoir trout rod, of about 9 feet 6 inches, with an extension handle, so that the butt of the rod can be tucked into your body when you have to play a fish and the reel handles kept well away from the danger of catching in your clothes when the fish runs. Have plenty of backing on the reel too, just in case. A small torch, a priest, waders, the big net, a game bag with coffee and sandwiches, and a box of flies are about all you will need. I like to have two rods, one with a floating line for the 1 inch tubes, another with a sinker for the large lures of 2 inches or more.

If you haven't explored the pools beforehand, choose the shallow side of a long deep pool where the water flows out from a deeper side by the opposite bank. By mid-August get there at about eight o'clock, knowing it will be dark at nine, and wait by the side of the pool, trailing your leader and your fly—maybe a 1 inch Stoat's Tail with a silver body—in the water, so that, when you start fishing, the nylon, well-soaked, will not show on the surface.

Bats will soon be coming out to hunt for insects. In Ireland they say 'if you see three bats it's time to start fishing', but I like to wait longer, until the vegetation on the far bank becomes a blur. Suddenly you will hear a splash. They're here! A big sea trout comes up straight out of the water and drops back. Further upstream a salmon lunges. A sea trout comes straight up out of the water, very neatly, and then bashes down.

Now is the time to start. Wade out very very gently. No ripples. No noise. Cast your fly to the far bank and let it swing round into the shallows. And again! You feel a pluck! That is a sea trout. Go on casting. On the third cast he takes properly and this time you have him. Standing where you are, without moving, you may take as many as two or three fish from the same pool. Fascinating fishing! The best of it comes in the first hour or so after dusk. If, suddenly, the rises stop, then change over from floating line to the rod with the sinking line and the large lure. Although the pool suddenly goes dead if you persist with the sinker you may well take one of the big fish which have been lying low.

But the sea trout, being on their spawning run, like the salmon, are also unpredictable in their behaviour. One night you may take four or five fish and the next morning you may invite a friend to come with you because the fish are in and taking, yet when you go out that night neither of you will have a touch. These fish have moods which no one has yet been able to explain.

ROY BUCKINGHAM

*

Success with the Sea Trout

WE ARE lucky in Devon and Cornwall. Practically every river except the Exe, has a good run of sea trout. The local name for them is peal, and the smaller fish that shoal up in August are known as harvest peal, but the big peal are getting to be called sea trout these days. They are all the same fish, coming up river from mid-summer onwards to the spawning grounds, and some of them are very big, over 10 lb, even in the smaller rivers like the Tiddy which runs into the sea near Devonport.

Night fishing is the best way of taking sea trout and the deadliest method is with the fly. I'm no purist about that. I'd fish other ways if I thought they were better but they're not. There is a further thing about fly fishing. You need to exercise considerable skill and to think hard to fish a fly well and that's also what I like doing.

The early part of the season is best—the high mid-summer run—which is roughly from the end of June through July and August but not much after that because the autumn fish are heavy with spawn and should be let through, and their flesh is pale and tasteless by comparison with high summer fish.

Before we start talking about how to catch sea trout on the fly I always think it right to give a word of warning. People who come down to fish West Country rivers for sea trout have preconceived ideas of how to fish, sometimes from their experience in other parts of the world, sometimes from reading books, and they often feel puzzled when they put these ideas into operation and things don't go right. They'll come back and say 'there's no fish in the river', which I know is not true because I've either caught fish myself the previous night or seen them that day shoaling up in the pools; or else they'll say 'there's fish there but they're not taking', and that's more difficult to argue against because it does happen sometimes, but not often, and what I suspect happens is mostly they've been using the wrong flies and the wrong methods of presentation.

Most of the problems that people have really boil down to casting faults of one kind or another. It's most surprising, because everything feels different at night, and almost everyone is inclined to speed up their casting in the dark without realising it. The result is splashy casts, the line falling in a heap and not straightening sufficiently in time to hook the fish on a take, and the tangling up of flies and leader, especially if you are using droppers. I've known very experienced fishermen do the wrong thing at night without realising it. So that is the first thing to deal with. Bad casting in the dark. There's only one way of doing it: go out to the river at night—but *not* the sea trout pools—and practise and practise until you get the feel. Before you are really proficient use a leader with only one fly. Don't use droppers until you *know* you can handle them.

When you have booked a beat for the night, always try to explore it cautiously during the day, peering over the bank, taking cover, watching for signs of fish, a flash of silver, a rise, faint grey shadows lying almost motionless under overhanging bushes or other cover. Local knowledge is always a great help in pointing out the holding pools but if there is no one to guide your choice of water look for a longish pool with a slow current in the middle, a nice shallow run in, and a slow shallow glide out to a gravelly tail. When you explore, work out how you are going to fish it. Watch out for trees that will hang up your back cast, for good places to stand and cover the pool, and if you have to wade—don't unless it is absolutely necessary—look out for the dangerous places.

For night fishing you need a 9 foot rod of an easy action, not stiff, that will give nicely to a heavy take. The sea trout can take very savagely and react violently so that a stiff rod may sometimes lead to a smash. An easy-actioned rod bends to a take but is quite firm enough to set the hook. I use a double-tapered floating line up to about a number 7 and a leader with two droppers. Remember, however, not to use droppers until you have the rhythm of night casting. I also carry another spare leader, already made up, in a cast carrier in a plastic box so that I can do a quick change with my flies. That is important. Sea trout are unpredictable, like salmon, and sometimes they will take only one type of fly presented in one way, and the next night won't look at it, so you always have to be prepared to change flies and change the method of presentation. We will go into that in a moment.

The flies I normally use are pretty well standard patterns, nothing special about them at all, but in West Country rivers, which often have a slight staining in them even in low water, it is important to use heavily dressed flies. Very thin patterns, which are good elsewhere, seem much less effective in our waters. For example, when I use a Zulu I want a good thick black woollen body, one hackle for the palmering to the tail, another hackle for the throat. That is what I mean by heavily dressed. The same with another good sea trout fly, the Invicta, which must have a good thickly dubbed yellow seal's fur body.

On my top dropper I use something like a size 12 Jungle Alexandra, the body of flat silver tinsel, the wings of green peacock herl with jungle cock cheeks instead of the usual red ibis. On the middle dropper a size 8 or 10 white-winged Coachman or a Peter Ross. Then unless it is bright moonlight, a really big fly on the point. This can be a 1 inch black tube fly, or a size 6 longshank Black Lure, or the heavily dressed Zulu. Remember that for good casting you must always have your heaviest fly on the point, for the heaviest fly will travel fastest when being cast.

If there is a bright moon then I am inclined to fish smaller flies but if these are to work well in the water and show a flicker of life then you need to fish a fine leader of about 5–6 lb breaking strain; normally I would never go much below 8–9 lb breaking strain because the take is often very fierce; indeed I have known good fishermen broken on a take with a 10 lb leader if they have been using a fairly stiff rod. There is nothing quite like the power of a fresh run sea trout. If you have to fish fine then you need a good quality reel with a light check and plenty of backing. Even on a small river like the Lyd I have had a 4 lb peal take all my line and 15–20 yards of backing on the first run. Never under-estimate these fish. They are very powerful indeed.

Other equipment: a lantern to take with you for major repairs or to see your way down to the river, a small pencil torch which you can hold in your mouth to change flies or leaders, and a bass to hold your fish. Never leave trout lying on the bank or a mink will have them and if the fish is in a bass they will carry that off as well! Put a string on the bass, tie it around your waist, loop it over your shoulder or hang it from a branch of a tree.

Landing nets: I do not trust those folding triangular nets, especially in the dark. A folding net with a fixed ring is much better or else a net on a fixed handle and loop which you can sling over your shoulder on a cord or strap.

Always travel light, with cast carrier and fly boxes in your pocket, and don't put things down in the dark, such as a waterproof jacket you're carrying with you, because you will leave it and not remember where you put it, so have to shine your torch all over the place. As a general rule, do *not* shine your torch on the water; yet once my fishing companion did just that, there was a splash, I cast towards it, and the sea trout took. There are always exceptions to the rule.

Some people, especially coming from the towns, are scared of the dark, though often they don't expect to be. I'll tell you some stories about that in a moment. But if you are not used to the country and its night noises then try and get someone to fish the pools with you. A husband and wife I know who come fishing on our water always carry a whistle on a cord and if they are into a big fish and need help or even if they are just feeling lonely they whistle to each other in the darkness. It's a great comfort, so they say.

Well, now. Let us suppose you have a beat for the night. There are two or three pools that you know, or at least expect, to hold fish. Reserve two of those pools to be fished after dark, knowing in advance where you are going to stand, where you have to avoid trouble on your back cast. The third pool you can fish, as we say, between lights, or just as it is beginning to get dark. Often that time between lights can be the best part of the day for taking fish. Don't despair if the mist is down. Often it will lift during the night and there are times when fish will take even in a mist, though you must not expect a good catch with mist on the water.

Fish the run into the pool first. This will often produce a peal in the fast water just before dark, and if you are lucky it could be a salmon. It doesn't happen often but I do know of several salmon taken in this way during dead low water levels. After fishing the run in, move and cover the middle of the pool quickly and then go down to the tail and fish. By this time it will be dark and you go on to the other pools.

When you are fishing don't start off by whacking your fly at the end of a 20 yard line into the far bank. You can have fish almost right under your feet. Cast a short line first of all downstream, below you, and then on the next cast fan it across a few feet, the same with the next; then take out more line and cast below you again, and repeat the process, always fanning out the fly, never covering exactly the same water.

This, of course, is where you come into casting problems. I remember one very good trout fisherman whom I took out after dark for the sea trout. He cast beautifully well to begin with and then, quite suddenly, I could hear his line dropping on the water with a splash. I had to give him a casting lesson at midnight and after that he caught a 3-pounder! His trouble was that he had gradually and without knowing it speeded up his false casting. He was stripping in too much line instead of lifting it off the water by raising his rod, and with only two or three feet of line outside the rod tip he had to false cast faster and with more effort to get enough weight of line out to allow him to shoot line properly. As a result, he had something which looked rather like a bunch of knitting at the end of his line. We had to cut off the leader and start again.

Another problem you have at night is taking the rod too far back on the back cast without knowing it. This causes the line to straighten out too high in the air on the forward cast which means it then springs back on you and falls in a heap on the water. It may be only slight and in the darkness you will not be aware of it but what it means is that the fly floats slowly downstream and looks like a piece of leaf or some other bit of debris in the water. While this is happening all that you are doing at the other end of the rod is retrieving slack line without having any or little effect on the fly at all. If the current is slow, and it often is in the mid-pools, your chance of catching a fish is practically nil. You may perhaps feel a tiny pluck but that's all. If the fly had been fishing properly, on a taut line, you would have had a strong take and hooked the fish. I know that this sounds like beginners' stuff but I have seen many experienced salmon and trout fishermen casting badly in the darkness without knowing it, not realising for one moment that they are doing anything different from the way they are fishing in the daytime.

Sometimes, of course, you will feel a pluck at the fly even when your line is taut and you have good tension on it. This generally means that the trout has plucked at the wing or the tail without touching the hook. Very annoying. In such cases you might try a smaller fly second time round but don't waste too much time on the same stretch of water. How fast should you retrieve the fly? Providing you have good line tension a slow retrieve is quite good enough, but vary this according to conditions, the speed of the water, and how you *feel* your fly is fishing.

Let us suppose you have been down the pool once with a heavy fly on the point, a 6 longshank Black Lure or something of that kind. There are no takes, no touches, nothing, but you have heard the thumping splash of a fish in the darkness so you know they are there. Change your leader or change the point fly and instead of having a heavy wet fly on the point try a floating fly. I like the ones that are made of deerhair such as a Muddler Minnow, a G and H Sedge, or a Rat-faced MacDougal. All these are natural floaters because of the buoyancy of the hair. Hugh Falkus puts a cork on the hook and calls it a Wake Fly. It is the same thing, the same principle.

Why bother to change? Very often a fish can see a fly better if it is looking upwards towards the light sky above it. It can certainly see the fly better if the fly is creating a wake, making V-shaped ripples on the surface as it is being retrieved by the angler across the current of the steam. That is the principle of the wake fly, whatever it is made of.

So the point fly is now a floater and makes that tell-tale ripple on the surface under tension and during the retrieve. Don't bother to change the other flies, the two droppers, unless you feel like it. I rarely change them myself so long as I feel that their size is about right—that is smaller flies during moonlight than on dark nights.

About droppers. As I say, don't use them unless you are confident you can be in complete control of your casting rhythms in the dark. I like to use them myself and when I am fishing a pool where there are no serious snags I am happy with an ordinary knotted leader. If there are snags in the pool then I use a knotless tapered leader with the droppers attached to it by a half-blood knot. If a trout takes a dropper then the dropper will slide down to the point fly so that the chance of snagging is reduced. By the way, always keep your lengths of nylon on the dropper short as you can to prevent them tangling around the main leader.

Kingcups – and an upstream cast for trout
of the Taw. (*Peter Keen*)

ABOVE Rough water on the Tamar – Conrad Voss Bark side-casting to avoid the overhanging trees. (*Peter Keen*)

BELOW Robin Lemon and the Woolly Worm at Wimbleball. (*Peter Keen*)

Evening rise at Blagdon. (*Peter Keen*)

Roy Buckingham takes a sea trout of the
Lyd – the white dots on the picture are
moths and flies illuminated by the flash.
(*Peter Keen*)

The 250-year-old cockpit at the Arundell
Arms Hotel is now the Rod Room – David
Pilkington (*centre*) with two of the guests,
Janice Morley and her brother Peter. (*Peter Keen*)

In the ring of the rise. (*Peter Keen*)

A well-known Devon trout fisherman of 60 years ago – G. Garrow Green, contributor to *The Field* and the *Fishing Gazette*, dressed for the moors in the fashion of the 1920s, greased army boots, Norfolk jacket, a worm tin on his belt, a fly box in his pocket, rod and net and wicker creel, and as like as not a flask of whisky at his hip. And RIGHT is a view of the kind of tackle of the time that still survives, the greenheart rod dating from 1905, and the kind of trout he would have been taking on Erme and Avon, Axe and Teign. (*Peter Keen*)

BELOW   Anne Voss Bark fishing the weir pool
of the Tamar at Gunnislake. (*Peter Keen*)

The curious dazzle of rippling water. (*Peter Keen*)

The magic of Blagdon. (*Peter Keen*)

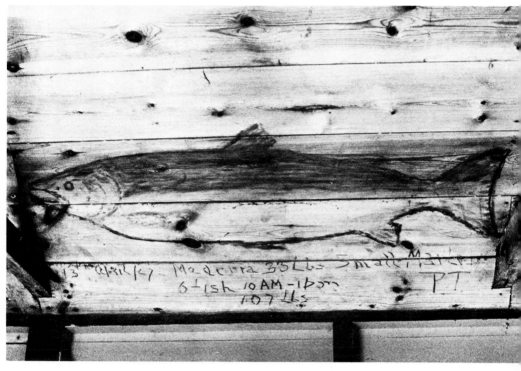

13ᵗʰ April/67 Madeira 33Lbs Small Martin PT
6 Fish 10AM-1pm
107 Lbs

BELOW   The ghillies. (*Peter Keen*)

Torridge salmon – visitors to the Half
Moon Inn at Sheepwash. (*Charles Inniss*)

ABOVE Concentration – a French visitor to
the Arundell Arms, Jean-Claude
Levandowski, taking cover as he stalks the
trout of the Carey. (*Peter Keen*)

Roy Buckingham showing the roll cast to a
beginners' class on the Arundell Arms
water of the Lyd. (*Peter Keen*)

High summer and low water – the
Monument pool of the Torridge below
Hele Bridge. (*Peter Keen*)

Wimbleball and an Exmoor pony. (*Peter Keen*)

Charles Bingham, mobile and
waterproofed, going for a salmon on the
Dart . . . and thinking again about the fly.
(*Peter Keen*)

A place where sea trout leap – the Golitha
Falls on the Fowey. (*Ray Bishop*)

Exmoor and the Barle. (*E.W.Tattersall*)

Two men in a boat at Blagdon. (*Peter Keen*)

'These enchanted valleys' – Dermot Wilson
fishing the dry fly on the Lyd. (*Dermot
Wilson*)

'The streams that curve down from the
moor' – the Barle above Dulverton.
(*John Tarlton*)

ABOVE The Blackbrook – one of Mike
Weaver's favourite pools, a short distance
upstream of the meeting of the Blackbrook
and the West Dart. (*Mike Weaver*)

A limit of twelve trout from the upper
Teign at Dunsford Wood Nature Reserve.
(*Mike Weaver*)

I rarely use a sinking line. Mostly you can get down deep enough on our rivers with an ordinary 9 foot leader on a floating line and it is so much nicer to fish the floater on our shallow streams; and even using a floating line I have found myself snagged under rocks on the bottom with a large single tube. A sinking line would only make things worse. The only time I find a sinker useful is when the river is fining down after a spate, with the water level above normal and the current going fast. If the water is like that, and that means coloured, then the only real chance of a sea trout is during the day and up until dark. Fishing in the dark in high and coloured water would usually be a waste of time.

I think that the use of floating lines applies to most of our best sea trout rivers, which I rank as being the Taw and Torridge, the Tamar, the Lyd and the Tavy, the Fowey and Camel, the Lynher and the Erme, though of course there may be a few very deep pools here and there where the sinker might do better, but as a rule I think not, and remember that even from a deep pool a trout will often come up quite a way to take the surface fly, especially the wake fly that advertises its presence by those big ripples on the water.

Sea trout can get really scared. They come up from the deep sea, running far upstream in a day and a night. I have caught them 18 miles above the tide with sea lice still on them. They come to rest in bright shallows, in brilliant sun, with strange movement all around. If you are going to fish for these wild scary creatures during the day you need a very stealthy and delicate technique.

I use my ordinary brown trout tackle, an 8 foot 6 inch rod, a light line and a very long leader, at least 13 or 14 foot long, needle-knotted on to the line to allow it to slip cleanly through the rings. It is very risky to fish light for these powerful fish but nevertheless your leader point must be as fine as a hair. I use about 3–4 feet of nylon of about 2½–3 lb breaking strain. Very light, you say? Maybe, but it can't be helped. You have to handle everything very very gently indeed and using nylon much thicker than that is certainly likely to put the fish off a take.

In daylight, sea trout seem to vary tremendously in their reactions to flies, far more so than they do at night, and sometimes their behaviour seems quite odd and unpredictable.

One day, when the river was dead low, it was full of fresh-run fish. They had just come into the pools. In deep water, about

20 yards above the tail of a long pool, I could see sea trout bulging. From the way they behaved, that distinctive bulge, you could tell they were taking nymph. Sea trout do eat in fresh water at times even though they have no need to do so.

I put on a Sawyer pheasant tail nymph and cast it to the rising fish. It was completely ignored. I tried the induced take, every tactic I could think of, but nothing at all happened. Yet there were the fish. Taking nymph. I didn't know what to do. I put on a wet-pattern Coachman, size 12, cast it above the rising fish and gave a slow retrieve in the slack water. Suddenly I saw a sea trout of about 2 lb following the fly down. There was a wonderful moment when I could have sworn it was going to take but it didn't and turned suddenly away, going back upstream with a flick of its tail. However, it was promising. I cast again and again and nothing happened, no response at all, no movement, yet I had not scared the fish. They were still rising.

Next time I cast well above the fish and allowed the Coachman to sink deep, hardly moving it at all. There was a silver flash in the water and the leader tightened. It was a good fish and I had two more on the same slow-sinking Coachman before the disturbance stopped the fish feeding. All those fish I took had their mouths full of nymph. Why should they refuse my artificial nymph and take a Coachman, which is really nothing like a nymph? I don't know. However, it is a useful method and one that I now use with great confidence, tying my Coachman with a little lead wire under the peacock herl. All the same I know perfectly well that it may work all right one day but not the next.

One day you will cast a very small dry fly, a size 16 or even smaller, across and up to a sea trout that is rising steadily and at once the whole shoal will move forward about a foot and then stop; and when that happens you know there will be no take from that lot. You have had it! Move on. The next day the same shoal won't be scared even by a whopping great lure dropped across their noses. That is what I mean by unpredictable.

A good tactic is to have a size 12 or 10 fly that has been heavily weighted with copper or lead wire to sink very quickly. A Coachman, or a Black and Peacock Spider, or a 14 longshank treble with plain copper wire on the shank and a black hackle on the throat. Cast this well above the shoal and let it sink deep. Give it one or two pulls or tweaks, then lift the rod as the fly comes downstream towards you. If you've got the movement right and in front and in sight of the shoal you may see as many as eight or ten fish following your fly downstream. Mostly it will be just curiosity but, sooner or later, if you are very careful in the presentation, one of them may have a go.

Another method to try is this: use a dry fly, same as you would for brown trout. Anoint your leader with mud or clay or sink-mix (a mixture of fuller's earth and detergent). The leader must sink at once. Cast upstream and across and skate the fly back to you, with the leader sunk, so that the fly only skitters back and over the surface of the water. A sedge-flutter kind of approach. It works well too when daddy-long-legs are on the water in August and September. Remember that none of these tactics work all the time, only some of the time.

It is at night though, away from all the odd things that happen in the day, that you will be most likely to take the really big fish. I think I ought to give a bit of a warning about night fishing, especially if you are from the towns and new to a particular river where you are going to fish. Share a beat. In the dark you can slip and fall and break an ankle. If someone else is fishing the river who knows you are there then sooner or later they will be with you. Otherwise you might have to sit out all night. It has happened.

But don't fish too close to anyone else. I remember a man fishing down from the top of a pool and his wife fishing up from the tail and both had a take at the same time. They played their 'fish' for quite a while before it gradually dawned on them that they had hooked each other's flies.

Seriously, it is a good thing to fish in pairs, especially if you're a townee and don't know the country. Shadows move. Things rustle in the undergrowth. You look over your shoulder. You're convinced someone is there. Heavy breathing. A form, a shape, in the darkness, coming towards you. You shine your torch. A cow. All the same your heart is thumping and your legs are weak. It is surprising how scared you can get if you are not used to the dark.

One man I knew was fishing a deep dark pool with high cliffs on either side when he saw something big and menacing moving on the water, coming upstream, coming directly towards him, something about 5 feet long making huge ripples. He said he thought his hair stood on end. Anyway, he shone his torch, the water exploded and mother duck and her brood of ducklings went off squawking downstream.

Foxes whistle, badgers snuffle, owls hoot and herons scream. Herons do other things as well. One fisherman on one of our rivers suddenly was aware of a hissing sound and, looking up, he saw a gigantic pair of wings flapping just above his head as a heron was coming in to land. He screamed. I think his first impression was that the devil had come for him. The bird screamed too. It jammed on its air brakes and took off almost from the poor man's head, pretty well emptying itself in terror as it did so. Heron droppings are large. They smell of fish. They are difficult to remove from clothes.

All the same, I love night fishing. I love the peace and quiet of it, the long silent pool glimmering in the faint light, the sudden splash of a big fish, the spreading ripples, the growing tension and excitement as you make your cast into the darkness. There is nothing quite like it anywhere.

A Fly by Night

The value of night fishing is as a sedative to fretted nerves and a tired brain. A sedative, yet something more, a portal of escape from the instancy of the present. As the night deepens the river takes command. Its voice mounts, filling the valley, rising to the rim of the hills, no longer one voice but a hundred. Time and place are dissolving; the centuries have lost their meaning; timelessness is all. One foot is crossing the invisible frontier which bounds the land of the old gods. Then comes the whistle of an otter, the bark of a fox—and you are back in the world of sentiency. Almost you fear to turn lest, black upon the moon-blanched sand, there should be the hoof marks of a goat.

T. C. KINGSMILL MOORE, *A Man May Fish*, 1960.

MIKE WEAVER

✤

Trout of the Moors

THE MOORLAND rivers of the south-west provide us with one of England's great strongholds of the wild brown trout, a commodity which is becoming increasingly difficult to find in a world of hatchery trout. Fishing a wild moorland stream, where the trout have never seen a hatchery, offers a special satisfaction which can never be matched on an artificially stocked river, no matter how good its fishing may be. When you catch a big moorland trout you know that you have deceived a wild creature that has survived for many years in spite of dangers from man and nature, while on more pampered waters your big fish may well have been fattening in a hatchery only a day before.

The fact that these moors hold huge stocks of trout is probably widely known, but what is not so well known is that careful fishing with the right method can produce catches of surprisingly good average size, with the occasional fish that would do credit to a chalk stream. And the right method for getting to grips with the better class of moorland trout is undoubtedly the dry fly.

Over fifty years ago, Kenneth Dawson commenced the chapter on dry fly in his classic *Salmon and Sea Trout in Moorland Streams* with the words 'of late years the dry fly has invaded the moorland and mountain streams which were once the inviolable sanctuary of the sunken lure, and there is no doubt in summer months that the former will at times kill far more fish, and those of a considerably greater average size, than could ever have been creeled by fishing wet'. Today I would go even further and say that, from the middle of April on, the dry fly will on *most* occasions take more and better moorland trout than the wet—certainly as far as the south-west is concerned.

So, where in the south-west can the dry fly angler cast for the wild brown trout of the moors? The best opportunities will be found on the streams that tumble down from the heights of Dartmoor and Exmoor, in the beautiful and often spectacular valleys of the two national parks. On Dartmoor the largest river system is that of the Dart, where the extensive Duchy of Cornwall fishery on the East and West Dart and their tributaries offer some of the least expensive fly fishing in England. Also on Dartmoor there are many more miles of water on the Teign, Avon, Tavy, Walkham and Plym. The Exmoor streams flow in two directions, with the Lyn descending quickly to the Bristol Channel and the Exe and Barle heading south to the English Channel. Between them, these streams provide a fantastic variety of opportunities for the dry fly man to practise his art.

Getting the best out of these rivers calls for a versatile approach to the dry fly, to meet the conditions that vary from river to river and, indeed, from one stretch to another on the same river. The popular view of a moorland stream is of fast flowing, boulder-strewn water and there are certainly many stretches of such water. However, there are also slower stretches where the accumulation of gravel and weed can give almost a chalk stream quality. One such reach on the Blackbrook, a tributary of the upper West Dart, can produce prolific hatches of duns and fine fishing to rising trout. The slow clear pools between the torrents of the East Lyn offer yet another challenge, as do the heavily bushed reaches of the upper Teign, where the novice can catch more trees than trout.

Although there will be times when there is enough fly on the water to make it possible to fish to rising trout, there will be many occasions when only the odd fish is showing and then you have to fish the water, and that raises the problems of locating fish. The moorland rivers hold a prolific head of fish, but they are certainly not spread evenly along the streams. In fact, there are long stretches where there are few fish worth catching and you have to learn which stretches give you a chance of catching trout of average size or better. The best way of all is to get out and fish a stretch of river regularly; this way you will gradually build up a knowledge of the best spots so that even on a day when there is not a rise to be seen, you will still be fishing the right places. Fortunately, trout favour the same water wherever you fish and once you have a knowledge of those spots which harbour fish it will stand you in good stead on most rivers.

It is particularly in the early weeks, when there are no rising fish to guide your casts, that you must stick to the right places. In the early part of the season, I look for a steady flow with a somewhat broken surface, between 2 and 4 feet deep. This will probably be in the top half of a pool and the fish will be somewhere between the full force of centre of the flow and the slack near the bank—not too fast and not too slow. At this time of the season, avoid the fast thin broken water which will probably hold only salmon parr or small trout, as will the slacks by the bank. The quiet tails of the pools, although they may hold fish, will be very difficult to fish as the trout will be lying deep and will scatter at the first cast. Some angling writers have recommended the slack water behind a boulder as a likely spot but my experience would suggest that worthwhile fish hardly ever lie in such a spot—if they did, how would they spot their food coming down with the current? However, they will often lie alongside a rock or in front of it.

When the river warms up and the fish are more active, it is possible to fish a much wider variety of lies. When there is really heavy insect activity and the fish are avidly seeking surface food, the normally difficult tails of the pool become fishable. The fish are so close to the surface and so pre-occupied with surface feeding that their usual extreme wariness in such spots is allayed.

You can also build up a knowledge of which stretches hold good fish by actually seeing them with the aid of a pair of polarising glasses, especially on a bright sunny day when the rivers are low and clear. Unfortunately, the fish will probably see you at the same time and rush off in fright, but you will learn which spots to approach carefully next time.

The trout streams of the south-west open for fishing on 15 March, at a time when the high moors can easily be still in the grip of winter. The rivers are likely to be high, unless the winter has been unusually dry, and certainly on the main streams conditions are unlikely to be suitable for the dry fly. However, the topmost reaches and tributaries of a moorland river drop very quickly and on any warm and relatively windless day it is worth trying the floater right from the start of the season. Cherry Brook on Dartmoor has given me some good sport with the dry fly in late March, as has the upper East Dart.

By the middle of April, with the first leaves appearing, the dry fly can be fished with every expectation of success on the main streams also. Fly hatches may still be sparse but most days will see an emergence of some Large Dark Olives (*Baëtis rhodani*) and, in the case of the Teign, there will always be the odd Grannom (*Brachycentrus subnubilus*) fluttering over the surface. Both of these insects are popular with the trout and it is a great pity that on the moorlands they rarely produce hatches sufficiently prolific to generate a big rise, but they frequently encourage the odd fish to rise steadily. An insect which does hatch in prolific numbers in the spring is the Stonefly (*Plecoptera*) but what a useless creature it is as far as the dry fly angler is concerned. Over the years I have seen countless thousands of Stonefly hatching on the moorland rivers, a phenomenon which is always met with total indifference by the trout.

From the middle of May until the end of June we can expect the cream of the dry fly on Exmoor and Dartmoor. This is the time when more riverside insects, whether aquatic or terrestrial, are more active than at any other time of the season. Of the ephemeroptera, the Olive Upright (*Rhithrogena semicolorata*) will be most noticeable, both in numbers and sizes. It will often hatch steadily over a long period and it is easily recognised—it is slightly larger than a Dark Olive and considerably lighter in tone. There will also be hatches of Pale Watery (*Baëtis bioculatus*), particularly on the West Dart where I have seen big hatches of this insect on the right day. The largest ephemerid normally seen on the moors is the Large Brook Dun (*Ecdyonurus torrentis*), but it hatches in such small numbers that it is hardly worth imitating. The Mayfly (*Ephemera danica*) is not a native of the moors but the very occasional specimen will be seen in some of the slower stretches.

Terrestrial insects are now really coming into their own, especially on the wooded Teign and Lyn, where the trees provide a constant flow of beetles, caterpillars and wood ants. But above all, there is the wonderful reliable Black Gnat. In a dozen years on the Devon streams I have never known this insect to fail, and the fish can always be relied on to take it avidly. This is the genuine *Bibio johannis* of May and early June, not one of the many small black flies which are often given the same name by mistake. Its close relation *Bibio marci*, the Hawthorn, can bring a flurry of activity when it is blown on the water.

A variety of Sedge (*Tricoptera*) species will be becoming increasingly evident and certainly well worth imitating. Unfortunately, the rivers of the moor do not seem to get the exciting late evening hatches that bring such explosive action on lowland rivers like the lower Exe.

In late June the hatches of Blue-Winged Olive (*Ephemerella ignita*) will be increasing and will continue off and on for the rest of the season. This will be mainly afternoon and early evening activity—not the late evening action of the chalk and limestone streams. This will provide the one opportunity for spinner fishing when the Sherry Spinners come back to the water. I have never seen the imago of any other ephemerid fall on the moorland streams in sufficient numbers to create its own rise.

By September, insect activity can become sparse and trout fishing can often be disappointing. From May through to August there will usually have been the odd rising trout to cast at but in September you will frequently be back to fishing the water if you are to make a good catch or two before the season ends on the last day of the month.

For many years I have used the lightest possible equipment for dry fly fishing—a day on the moors can involve many miles of walking and any weight that you can save in the choice of tackle will really be appreciated at the end of a long warm day. Most of my dry fly fishing is done with a four or five line. A suitable rod of 7 or $7\frac{1}{2}$ feet, in modern materials, need never exceed $2\frac{1}{2}$ oz; if it does, then the fittings are too heavy. My own preference is for a rod with a fast action and a weight-forward line; combined with a steep-taper leader, this outfit gives precision casting, even when it has to cope with the breezes which are a frequent feature of moorland fishing.

In nearly thirty years of fly fishing I have never been able to fish with a bag hanging from my shoulder so the introduction of the fishing waistcoat was a godsend. In it I carry my fly boxes, nylon for replacing leader points, floatant, hook sharpener, polarising glasses, licences, insect repellent, priest and nail clippers for cutting nylon. My landing net is aluminium hoop with a plastic handle and an elasticated loop; it cost a pound twenty years ago and, with no moving parts, should be good for another twenty years. In spite of my quest for weight saving, I frequently permit myself the luxury of a wading staff. The bed of a moorland stream can be rough and the security of three points of contact has to be experienced to be believed.

In *Salmon and Sea Trout in Moorland Streams*, Kenneth Dawson recommended only three patterns in the chapter on the dry fly—Blue Upright, Coch-y-Bondhu and, his favourite, Red Quill. With these three flies you could easily cope with most requirements over the course of a season, but many would add the Pheasant Tail and Greenwell's Glory to the list of standard patterns—and one of my favourites is the Half Stone. Size 16 will be the most useful for all of these flies, with some tied on 14s and 18s, and all of mine are tied without any wings.

The dressings which I use for these standard patterns are as follows. First the Blue Upright, one of the greatest flies to come out of Devon, and a good general representation of a number of duns when tied in a variety of sizes. A 16 will be about right when Dark Olives or Blue-Winged Olives are hatching—or when just fishing the water with no particular hatch taking place. An 18 with a really dark hackle will do for the occasional emergence of the Iron Blue—what a pity this insect is so rare on the moors—and an 18 or even 20 with a pale hackle for the Pale Watery. Here is the usual dressing:

Tail: Steely blue cock
Body: Stripped quill from the peacock eye feather; one side of the quill should be distinctly darker than the other to give a segmented body
Hackle: Steely blue cock

The dressing for the Coch-y-Bondhu is as follows. The genuine Coch-y-Bondhu hackle may be hard to find and I am quite happy to use a brown hackle with a black hackle wound through it.

Body: Two or three strands of bronze peacock herl, twisted
Hackle: Coch-y-Bondhu cock

Peacock herl bodies can be rather brittle and begin to fall apart after a few fish have been taken so I take a couple of precautions to give added strength. First of all, apply some varnish to the hook shank before winding the herl and, for added security, wind a ribbing of fine black silk.

Next the Red Quill, the procedure for which is very similar to the Blue Upright:

Tail: Red cock
Body: Stripped quill from the peacock eye feather
Hackle: Red cock

The Pheasant Tail is another hackle pattern, and especially valuable when there are any spinners on the water. I often use a medium blue dun hackle and tail, instead of the usual honey dun.

Tail: Honey dun cock
Body: Herl from a pheasant centre tail feather with rib of fine gold wire
Hackle: Honey dun cock

The Greenwell's Glory is one of the all-time favourites and I like this hackle pattern given by Courtney Williams in *A Dictionary of Trout Flies:*

Tail: Furnace cock
Body: Yellow silk, well waxed, ribbed with fine gold wire
Hackle: Furnace cock and medium blue dun cock

The Half Stone, like the Blue Upright and Pheasant Tail, originated in Devon, where it remains a popular wet pattern. The dry dressing which I use is as follows:

Tail: Blue dun cock
Body: Yellow or primrose silk or floss for rear half, with dubbed mole fur for the front half
Hackle: Blue dun cock

Another outstanding pattern is the small hair-wing sedge, which is one of my standard offerings from late May until the end of the season if nothing specific is hatching. I tie a variation of Skues Little Red Sedge, as follows:

Body: Dark hare's ear, ribbed with fine gold wire
Wing: Grey-brown deer hair, lying back over the body
Hackle: Deep red cock
Hook: 16

The buoyant deer hair ensures that this fly is an excellent floater and the body hackle often used in sedge patterns is unnecessary.

On the moorland streams it is unusual for a hatch of a single insect to be sufficiently prolific to result in the trout becoming pre-occupied but the exception comes in the late May and early June of each year when that wonderfully reliable insect, the Black Gnat, emerges in countless millions. The great virtue of the Black Gnat is its presence for most of the daylight hours and the opportunity for many hours of steady feeding by the trout. This is a time for an accurate representation of the natural insect and the following dressing is both effective and visible to the angler:

Body: Black fur or synthetic substitute
Wing: White, feather fibre or fine hair, lying back over the body
Hackle: Black cock
Hook: 18 or 20

For much of the season, especially on tree-lined streams like the Teign and Lyn, beetles are a regular part of the trout's diet and a suitable representation really earns its keep. The Coch-y-Bondhu is, of course, one of the oldest beetle imitations, and I frequently use it, but my preference is for the all-deer-hair beetle in the American style, with black and brown versions on 16 and 18 hooks. This beetle is realistic, floats well and catches fish, especially in low-water conditions when fish are being selective.

For many years I tied all my dry flies on the Mustad 94840 and found it a most reliable hook. More recently I have turned to the barbless hook and now use the Mustad 94845. The lack of a barb makes it easier both to hook and unhook fish. Over the course of a season on the moors I return around a thousand trout so anything that ensures that the fish go back in good condition is well worthwhile.

After more than a dozen years of fishing the fly on Dartmoor and Exmoor, I am very aware that there are many stretches, and indeed whole rivers, which I have yet to fish. Inevitably, we all return frequently to those reaches which have given us good sport, when perhaps we should be exploring new waters. On the following pages I have selected a variety of days on a wide range of waters in an attempt to illustrate the varying challenges and opportunities which face the moorland angler, and how I have tried to deal with them. Inevitably, these examples are drawn from days when the fish were responsive and the sport was above average—who wants to read about hours of fruitless endeavour? However, such days are by no means exceptional and anyone who really gets to know the moorland streams of the south-west can hope for a good percentage of successful outings, and should settle for nothing less.

My local river is the Teign and I am fortunate to live in the middle of the 12 mile stretch which is controlled by the Upper Teign Fishing Association. With so much fishing on my doorstep I could select many examples of memorable days of trout fishing on this picturesque river, but a day in 1980 provides an example of fine fishing and an opportunity which comes all too infrequently.

Around the middle of May in 1980, the woods of the Teign valley suffered—or enjoyed, depending on your point of view—a positive plague of looper caterpillars. These small lime-green creatures of less than an inch in length fell upon the newly emerged foliage with relish and the leaves of bankside trees were quickly reduced to skeletons. With such vast numbers present, many caterpillars inevitably found their way into the river, thus presenting the trout with their greatest feast for seasons. I first became aware of this phenomenon when cleaning a fish which was positively crammed with loopers—so full that the lime green colouring glowed through the stomach wall.

This was obviously an opportunity not be be missed so I tied up half-a-dozen simple imitations of the looper, consisting of a size 10 hook with lime green fluorescent wool tied from the eye to nearly half way around the bend. A very basic pattern, but it immediately found favour with the trout.

For the next two or three weeks I took large catches of trout with greater ease than I can ever remember. At any time of day the fish were eagerly awaiting the looper. It was not even necessary to cast accurately as the distinct 'plop' produced by the arrival of this heavy lure on the water frequently attracted trout from a yard or more away. Furthermore, the trout were much more widely spread than usual with the shallow still tails of the pools fishing as well as the normally more productive quicker water nearer the head.

Most of these catches were made around Fingle Bridge but on the first day of June I drove downstream and parked the car below Clifford Bridge. I then walked a further mile downstream through the Dunsford Wood Nature Reserve and over the next two hours fished back upstream to the car. The trout were still taking the looper avidly and the two hours produced twenty-five fish between 8 and 11 inches. I rarely keep more than a brace of fish but on this occasion I retained a limit of twelve, and half of them were over 10 inches, an unusually high average for the Teign. Two days later the loopers were gone for that year.

My favourite stretch of really small stream fishing is on the last mile of Blackbrook before it joins the West Dart. Most of this water is relatively slow flowing and often weedy, which explains the fact that on this piece of water I have experienced bigger hatches of fly than anywhere else on Dartmoor. Here I have enjoyed fine fishing in hatches of Dark Olive, Pale Watery and Blue-Winged Olive—and it is the last which provided one of my most memorable outings in 1981. On chalk and limestone rivers, the BWO is very much a creature of late evening, but on Dartmoor the best hatches are often in the afternoon and this was just such an occasion. I had arrived at Prince Hall at noon on a warm overcast day in July and set off up the West Dart with high hopes. An hour later I reached the mouth of Blackbrook having worked hard for only a couple of 7 inch trout. As I moved up the first few yards of the brook I became aware of a trickle of BWO duns—a trickle which quickly became a full-blooded hatch. Almost immediately the day was transformed, the previously undisturbed surface now broken by eagerly rising trout.

If this had been evening I would have tied on the traditional Orange Quill but in daytime a more natural representation of the insect usually does better so I tied on a fly with olive green body and dark blue dun hackle on a 16 hook. The fish took this without hesitation. In less than two hours I netted eighteen trout between 8 and 14 inches, many of the fish coming from tiny pockets among the weeds in only a few inches of water.

Although this was an exceptional hatch, the Dartmoor angler should always keep his eye open for emerging insects and respond quickly to any opportunities which they offer. Earlier in the same season, this same stretch of Blackbrook gave me an exciting hour on an otherwise quiet day with a hatch of Dark Olive.

I have fished the East Lyn on a few occasions only over the past three years but already it ranks as one of my favourite streams. The part that I know best is around Rockford, which marks the top of Watersmeet Fishery and the bottom of the Glenthorne Fishery, both of which are controlled by the South West Water Authority. Below Rockford the Lyn quickly drops into its spectacular wooded gorge with large, often still pools linked with rushing cascades. On a bright day the quiet water at the tail of such a pool is like an aquarium with large numbers of small to moderate fish cruising around. Nearer the head of the pool, where the water is quicker, the fish will be bigger and more catchable, providing they can be approached from the high banks without scaring them.

Upstream of Rockford, the Lyn breaks out of the gorge and runs between a mixture of woodland and meadow. Here the long steady runs are ideal for the dry fly. On my last visit there were myriads of Black Gnat over the water and in every run or pool the trout could be seen lying just below the surface, sipping the little dark flies. The size 18 imitation took many trout that day, as it had on previous visits at that time. If you want a day of Black Gnat fishing at its best, try the Glenthorne Fishery in late May or early June.

Free fishing is hard to find these days but it still exists in places, and one such place is on the upper reaches of the Devon Avon, from Shipley Bridge up to Avon Dam. This 1½ mile stretch runs through open moorland and there is no charge for anyone holding a Water Authority licence—and that includes fishing the reservoir too!

Most of this stretch is shallow but the upper part has a number of deep pools between low granite cliffs to offer variety. There are plenty of wild trout around 8 inches, with the occasional 10-incher to make things interesting, and the fish on this stream are really free rising. This really is a lovely place to spend two or possibly three hours working your way upstream with a dry fly. The only snag is that it is a popular spot for visitors. Try to fish it during the week.

When I came to live in Devon, the first river that I fished was the West Dart and it remains one of my favourites. It can be moody but when conditions are right the fishing is first class. The biggest trout I have ever had from it was just an ounce short of three pounds. Not so bad for a wild trout of the moors!

THE DAY OF THE OLIVE QUILL

*In the Easter holidays I went alone once or twice to the Dart.
I do not know how the Dart fares now, for it is nearly twenty
years since I have seen it; but in those days there was beautiful
trout water between Staverton and Buckfastleigh, which
could be fished by ticket, and if one was not disappointed by
trout of less than half a pound, there was very good sport to be
had. I remember once fishing a part of the river where there
was a succession of streams, which towards the middle of the
day seemed alive with little trout, rising actively all over the
water at natural flies. It was one of those maddening days
when the trout rise in quantities and take no notice of the
artificial flies. I could do nothing and the other anglers below
and above me, of whom two or three were in sight, were not
doing very much better. At last in despair I waded out and
went down to a smooth piece of the river between wooded
banks. In this place the water was clear and varied from a foot
to perhaps three feet in depth. No one was fishing and trout
were rising in shoals and very quietly. A stout March Brown,
such as I had been using above, would have put them all to
flight, but the trouble with using a dry fly for each separate
trout seemed out of proportion to the size of the fish. Yet as I
wanted very much to save an empty basket I put on one small
Olive Quill and waded in quietly below the rising fish. They
took the little dry fly as if they were pleased to see it and when
the rise was over I waded out with thirty-one trout in my
basket. The old angling diary to which I have referred gives
the weight of the largest at eight ounces.*

*As I emerged from the trees on the bank I met one of the
best of the local anglers returning from above with a lighter
basket than usual. He stopped me and asked what I had done.
I told him and he then asked to see the fish. I opened my
basket. 'You can't have caught these today with the fly', he
said. 'Yes' I replied; 'I caught them with a dry fly'. 'Dry fly',
he said very sternly, 'we know nothing about a dry fly here'.
Then he went on his way, with thoughts, I fear, that were not
very kind.*

VISCOUNT GREY OF FALLODON, *Fly Fishing*, 1899.

So give me a light trout rod and the dry fly, and a stream which runs clear through moor or meadow, and I ask no more of the day.

LORD HOME, *Border Rivers*, 1979.

A PLACING OF FLIES

On a little river, you have to be canny. It is all a question of where you put your fly. The shorter your line—and the time you play your fish—the better. And you have to know water; the tempting deep places which seem almost unable not to produce a fish are usually as unprofitable as fishing a ditch. But there is a long innocent stretch on the little Exe, for instance, where a line of great old oaks stretch their branches far out over the water. And if you can get your line in under there you are almost always rewarded with a couple of fine fish, usually in remarkably good condition. I don't know why this should be except that these embarrassing oak branches hang over a long stickle, and the water at that point must be particularly rich with good trout food. At any rate, fish taken from there are nearly always the best you will get from that mile or so of river. Then, on the Barle, you can work up a narrow stretch that rushes under a main bridge. And here, if you can work your fly properly with the dense underbush on either side of you, you will get fish twice the size you will ever take from the more likely broader water lower down. Those who have fished that bit of water will know the stretches I am talking about. They will also know the broad stretch where Exe and Barle meet—to run down into the Black Pool— where you will hardly ever catch a decent trout.
NEGLEY FARSON in *Going Fishing*, 1942.

DERMOT WILSON

*

Trout of the Valleys

I HAVE fished the Hampshire chalk streams, particularly the Test and Itchen, ever since I was a boy. And that means nearly a lifetime, since I am not far from sixty now. So I suppose I have had an ample measure of what most people consider the cream of dry fly fishing, perhaps the best in the world.

For a dozen years or so my wife and I actually lived in a mill on a chalk stream, a delightful tributary of the Test which ran chuckling beneath our bedroom. 'Aren't you lucky?' was the invariable envious reaction from fishing friends.

And the chalk streams are indeed very dear to me. Yet every season I escape as often as I can to fish my dry fly on the enchanting little spate rivers of the West Country. I rate them just as highly for the sheer fishing pleasures they offer and in certain ways I prize them even more than the storied streams of Hampshire. I love them and can hardly bear to leave them when my visits end.

My discovery of the West Country as a source of fishing delight took place one year shortly after the Second World War. When I went down there, around the middle of April, I was feeling a little superior. I expected a change from my usual fishing haunts but after all, I told myself, I could hardly expect the fishing to be so challenging, let alone so good. I was soon to be dramatically disillusioned.

When I reached the banks of the Tamar not a rise was to be seen. So to pass the time I put on a Gold-Ribbed Hare's Ear and cast in towards a ripply run under my own bank. Almost as soon as it touched the water a trout rose, took it, dived under a tree root and broke the leader.

I was left gaping. Since then I have been left gaping a great many times by the side of various West Country streams. This was only a foretaste of the many surprises they had in store for me.

But back to that first day. I began to discover the joys of 'fishing the river' as opposed to 'fishing the rise'; they are different joys but no less exciting. When each successive cast may be the one that brings up a fat trout the suspense is continual. Some casts naturally seem to you to be better placed than others and when you've guessed right you always feel like patting yourself on the back, and deservedly so.

On this day, however, some fly started to appear after an hour or two and then indeed I found myself 'fishing the rise'. There was no shortage of rising fish. They sucked and splashed and dimpled all over the river. It was then that I completely lost my cool. I began casting frantically, to cover as many fish as possible, and inevitably started to fish badly. I must have lost a dozen flies in bushes through not taking the elementary precaution of frequently looking behind me. When my fly succeeded in landing on the water, it did so splashily. I didn't pay enough attention to drag. And I missed or pricked fish after fish.

I ended the day with four nice trout in the bag and a definite feeling of having been bested. I didn't dare try to work out my ration of trout caught to trout lost and trout missed. It would have been altogether too shaming. I went to bed full of ruses for doing better on the next day but, so far as I can remember, I don't think I did.

Admittedly I probably struck a good day for my first trial of the Tamar, a day when innumerable trout seemed ready to rise. But I have known even better days since then, as well as days that have been rather more dour. By the time my initial visit to the West Country was over, the lure of its dry fly fishing was deep in my being. I longed to return, to try my hand once more at those game and tricky trout, and to tread again the enchanted valleys I'd so quickly come to love.

The Tamar I enjoyed immensely, but before long I discovered that its tributaries held even more charm for me. And I still fish them in preference to the main river, whenever I can. Their smaller valleys are just a little more intimate, a little easier to feel at home in, a little more conducive to the sense of secluded happiness that fishing so often brings. The tributaries offer infinite variety too.

Instead of the big pools and long flats of the main river, every twist of the little streams—and goodness, how they twist!—reveals a new kind of water.

The two streams that I have fished most often are the Lyd and the Carey. The Lyd is quite a large tributary, rising in the heart of Dartmoor and joining the Tamar about two miles downstream of Launceston. As well as its resident brown trout, it has runs of salmon and sea trout. The Carey, by complete contrast, is a tiny winding stream with no salmon or sea trout, rising on the fringe of the moor near Beaworthy and flowing into the Tamar near Launceston. Surprisingly enough, although it is far smaller than the Lyd, its trout are just a little larger. I adore it.

The valleys of both streams have one value in common, a wild and enchanting beauty that sets them apart from the more manicured environment of the chalk streams. You feel here that nature has never been tamed or tampered with and that you are privileged to set foot in a scene that must have remained unchanged for hundreds of years. Yet they welcome you, these little streams. They do not seem to treat you as an interloper, but rather to patter out a warm invitation to you.

Here you will find no well-mown fishing paths, no comfortably equipped fishing huts, few indeed of the man-made aids and conveniences that cosset the chalk-stream fisherman. Getting into the water, or even to the water's edge, is often a tortuous business. Frequently you have to find or force your way down through thorn and bramble, carefully thwarting their constant desire to become entangled in your clothes, your line, your landing net.

If you hurry too much you will probably sustain a scratch or two, but ladies need not be alarmed. With caution a whole skin can be preserved.

Unless you are fishing with a companion you may well catch not a glimpse of another human being all day. Your most frequent fishing companions are in fact likely to be cows. I have a great weakness for cows. They seem to me to have found the secret of relaxed living, a secret which they share with many fishermen. One should never expect anything to hasten their leisurely pace. I am as impatient as the next man when my car is held up by traffic jams, but if it's held up by cows I can always take it in good part. I also invariably derive a kind of perverse pleasure if I come across a

Rolls-Royce hooting at a herd of ponderous cows as they saunter across the road.

You will see plenty of sheep as well in these valleys, but they never seem quite so interested in fishing. A sheep seldom spares a fisherman more than a passing glance. But a cow will often follow him down to the riverbank and watch critically, if expressionlessly, while he casts. Sometimes she may seem a nuisance, especially if she has girl friends with her, but cows hardly ever frighten trout so much as might be feared, since the trout are used to them. Whenever I do something clever in front of a cow, such as maybe catch a fish, I usually find myself looking towards her for approbation.

The trout in these streams are as wild and pretty as their settings. A word or two should be said about their size. Do not expect the 2- and 3-pounders of many chalk streams and still waters. Far from it. The trout of most West Country rivers run about three or four to the pound. The limit is 8 inches. (On Dartmoor it is only 6 inches.) But do not on any account despise these strong little fish, for they can be just as exciting as their bigger brethren.

It is all a question of matching your expectations to the stream. The transition occurs quickly and easily. I personally find it only natural, as soon as I hook a fish on the Lyd or Carey, to think on a smaller scale. 'Is it sizeable?' I wonder excitedly to myself, meaning 'Is it 8 inches or over?' An 8 inch Lyd trout in the net gives me as much of a thrill as a fish of two pounds from the Test. And occasionally, often enough to keep suspense at a high pitch, there's a half-pounder. A half-pounder! Such a trout can send the heart leaping into the mouth as readily as any fish I know.

Then there is all the thrill of the hunt that comes from fishing for wild fish. The sense of the hunt is part and parcel of fishing at its most enjoyable. For every year that man has farmed on this planet, he has hunted for at least ninety-nine years. The hunting instinct, whether we welcome it or not, is deeply etched into our make-up. And to indulge it to the full the quarry must be wild. Here the streams of the West Country can score a point against most of the famous fisheries of the south. The majority of the latter are of necessity stocked, since the reproduction of wild trout cannot keep pace with fishing pressure. There is little point in railing against stocked trout. They are inevitable in this day and age, and they give both sport and pleasure. But some waters are overstocked, stocked with too many fish, too frequently. It is difficult to feel like a mighty hunter if you have a shrewd suspicion that the trout you are casting for was put there a day or two ago simply to assuage your blood-lust.

You need have no such suspicions on a stream like the Carey. So far as quantity of wild trout is concerned, it is a better provider than the average chalk stream. It produces masses of trout and though they may not grow so big, it offers them an ideal natural habitat. Trout are easily its most common fish. (The most common fish in the chalk streams, perhaps surprisingly, is the bullhead— and in many stretches there are more grayling than trout.) Every trout you catch on the Carey is a true wild fish, born and bred in the wild little river.

They are all muscle too. Though by no means thin, they are often not so deep as the trout of slower waters. After all, they take more exercise. They have to keep their position in a brisk current and they have to work harder to find their food. This makes them exceptionally strong little fish, as you soon find out if you hook one. They fight as well as any trout and even an 8-incher will frequently take out line.

Furthermore they are good-looking fish, delightfully freckled and with frequent red spots. And they taste good too. A couple of these 'breakfast trout' are indeed a breakfast worth having. Add one or two more, and you have a truly splendid main dish for a meal. Or if you wish, smoke them and serve them as starters. You will not be disappointed by their flavour.

One delight of fishing West Country streams is that you need never use heavy or cumbersome tackle. A long rod is in fact a distinct nuisance, since it makes life difficult when you want to make short casts on overgrown stretches, manipulating your back-cast so that it goes under bushes and branches and not into them. A delicate wand of a rod is quite sufficient. Even though the larger rivers are fairly broad in places, you can nearly always with judicious wading avoid any necessity for a long cast. You will find plenty of trout within easy range.

Your rod, and of course you yourself, must however be capable of delicacy and accuracy. Delicacy is at a premium on small streams, since clumsiness usually spells disaster. A splashily presented fly in a confined space normally acts as a danger signal not only for the trout you are casting to, but quite possibly for several others as well. You may disturb many yards of water.

Accuracy is a *sine qua non* as well. Admittedly, on the larger streams, you will find long broad runs which may harbour trout all over their length and breadth, and where beginners can catch fish without having to be too accurate, but on the smaller rivers, like the Carey, these are few and far between. Trout will lie in small pockets and it takes accuracy to cover them. Accuracy also helps you to place your fly so as to avoid drag. An inaccurate cast, furthermore, can all too easily land your fly in some piece of overhanging greenery.

My own favourite rod is a dainty little cane, 6 foot 9 inches, rated to carry a no. 4 line. It's a delight to cast with all day, since it doesn't tire one in the least, and it'll reach just as far as anyone on these streams could ever wish. It's also a very handy rod for restricted places. Certainly I've never felt the need for anything bigger or more powerful.

The comparatively light, fine line is a help as well, or so I feel. It lands on the water with less disturbance than a heavier line and causes less line-shadow than a thicker line. This latter point may sound fairly academic, because theoretically you shouldn't be lining fish at all, but on these trout-filled streams there are often unnoticed fish lying between you and the trout you're casting to. The less you scare them the less chance there is of them darting upstream to frighten others.

I always use a 9 or 10 foot leader. A shorter one increases the likelihood of scaring fish and provided you use a needle-knot for attaching your leader to your line, the joint will slip quite easily through the rings of a short rod when you bring a trout to the net. I have indeed been tempted to use a longer leader but I find it difficult to manage in a wind. Here, as always, a contrary wind can be awkward and some skill at into-the-wind casting is a great advantage. Remember, do not force your cast, simply cut it down onto the water a little more finely, by finishing your forward cast rather lower than you normally would.

How fine should you fish? It is a bad practice to fish so fine that you continually break in trout, causing unnecessary distress by leaving flies behind. But these trout, strong though they are, should not really break you if you use a 5 × (or 3 lb) tippet or even 6 × (or 2½ lb) tippet. You just have to be careful with the strike.

Provided you do not break on the strike, it is surprising how much strain can be brought to bear on a trout even with nylon of no more than 2 lb test. A fairly fine tippet will serve you well on these streams, particularly in bright low-water conditions.

Now for flies. Insects make up the dominant proportion of a trout's diet in West Country streams, where the comparatively acid water is unsuitable for large populations of shrimp and snail and similar food. Even the insects are not so plentiful as in more alkaline waters. So by and large the trout have to take what they can get. By and large again, they are prepared to swallow whatever insect offers itself for consumption, and they are therefore fairly catholic in their tastes. At times, however, when there is a good hatch of one particular fly, they can be infuriatingly discriminating, but more often they will rise to a variety of offerings.

Another good reason for this is the diversity of the natural insects that the trout feed on. You will seldom find here the exclusive concentration on certain ephemerids that is such a feature of the behaviour of trout in chalk streams. Sedges, for instance, are more common in relation to ephemerids than they are on chalk streams. So are midges and stoneflies. And so are all manner of bugs and goodies, many of them terrestrial in origin, which may hatch or drop on the water—such as beetles, bluebottles, houseflies, ants, grasshoppers and caterpillars. And many others.

None of this means, however, that choice of fly is of no importance. Many flies may take trout, but on any one day there will usually be a few flies that consistently take more trout than others do. Your best guide for patterns will often be local advice.

Naturally I have my own favourites. Who hasn't? If I had to go through the agonizing process of reducing my West Country flies to six only, I think that these six would have to be: Gold-Ribbed Hare's Ear, Beacon Beige, Halford's Black Gnat, Little Red Sedge, Royal Wulff and Coch-y-Bondhu. But these would be followed pretty closely by Greenwell's Glory, Tup, Hawthorn, Coachman, Blue Upright, Half Stone, Black Palmer, Silver Sedge, Pheasant Tail, Grey Wulff, Olive Upright, Yellow Sally and Welshman's Button.

Then you may sometimes do well on more specialised flies when and where their natural counterparts appear. These will be flies such as Mayfly and Spent Gnat, Daddy-Longlegs, Black Ant, Red Ant and Green Grasshopper. Altogether your choice can be pretty wide. As always, it pays to inspect the water and to try to see what type of food the current is carrying to the trout. Remember one thing. It can change pretty quickly.

How big should your fly be? There are two considerations here. One is the size of the natural fly. And the other is visibility for the fisherman. Unless you can see your fly, especially in rough water, you may well miss seeing a trout rising to it, since the trout often makes very little surface disturbance when they take. Your only indication may be that one second the fly is there, and the next second it isn't. This magic disappearing trick is indeed one of the great excitements of dry fly fishing on a West Country stream.

So you should match the size of your artificial to the size of the natural if you can, but do not be afraid to exaggerate if your eyesight calls for it. Typical 'natural' sizes are about 12 for a Sedge, 14–16 for an Ephemerid and 18–20 for a Black Gnat. If you are casting to rising trout in smooth flats in pools you will be able to see smaller flies than if you were fishing in rough water. Or at least you will be able to see a rise where your fly should be. I have often gone down to a size 20 Black Gnat on smooth, slow water and have done better than with larger flies.

One other important factor is floatability. If your fly is too easily drowned by the ripples of the stream, you may well fail to see a take. You might as well in fact be fishing an upstream wet fly—which is a skilful and fascinating technique in its own right, but hardly your present object.

To a large extent the floatability of a fly depends on its dressing. To float as it should it must be well tied with good materials. Good springy hackles, for instance, are an essential. If you find a source of unexceptional flies, don't grudge them an extra penny or two per fly. Some patterns of fly are also more buoyant than others. Probably the most notable patterns for buoyancy and visibility are the flies in the Wulff series, of which the best-known are the Grey Wulff and Royal Wulff. Both can be very effective on West Country streams.

Take quite a lot of flies with you. I don't care if you are the finest caster in the world—you are bound to lose some. You will often be casting under or in between bushes and trees, all of which have a magnetic attraction for flies. Not surprisingly you will be more inclined to get hung up behind than in front, so glance frequently over your shoulder to see exactly how your back cast

will fare. In heavily wooded places roll-casting can be very useful
and is well worth learning to accomplish if you're unused to it. It
isn't difficult. But whatever you do, you will still lose flies. If you
can tie your own, of course, this won't cost you nearly so much as
if you can't.

As regards other tackle and paraphernalia, the optimum is
undoubtedly the minimum. The fewer things you have hanging
about your person, the less there'll be to catch in the undergrowth
as you scramble or step down into the river. That is one reason
why I prefer a fishing waistcoat to a bag. The article that always
seems to get caught up most frequently is your landing net. It
appears to seek out thorns and brambles with a single-minded
volition of its own. If you then tug at it too hard and impatiently
you're likely to tear the mesh. Nowadays I usually carry my
landing net in front of me when I make my way through bushes.
By doing this I can sometimes, though not always, avoid having to
interrupt my journey to extract the net from the environment.

The tactics of fishing a West Country stream deserve some
description, though on the whole they are simply common sense.
The great object, as always, is to avoid frightening your trout
before you have a chance to deceive him. As we fishermen walk
and wade upstream, I am sure that we disturb more trout than we
ever guess. They can be very shy, particularly in shallow water,
and even more particularly when the water is low and clear. A
touch of colour in the water, provided it is not enough to put fish
off the rise, sometimes helps a little.

I believe that the sight of a fisherman on the skyline, even if he is
some distance away, is especially likely to scare these trout.
Skylines should be shunned at all costs. If there is a bank or a tree
or a bush behind you, the trout will be far more disposed to let you
approach to within easy casting range. Here the bankside vegetation, even though it contributes to the loss of a few flies, can be a
boon. In fact you should usually be able to cast only a short line,
and this is as it should be. A long line, lying athwart the
cross-currents of the stream, is far more prone to cause drag. You
will also get hung up more often, and you will hook fewer of the
fish you rise.

As to the rest, the usual rules apply. If you are not wading, keep
reasonably low on the bank. Kneeling sometimes helps but is by
no means always necessary. It also helps a little if you can cast

horizontally, rather than vertically since the fish will then find it less easy to see either your rod or the flash of your rod. Never hurry upstream, or you will be sure to miss feeding fish. And when you wade, which will be frequently, do so slowly and gently. Try not to clump along, since trout are sensitive to vibration. Above all, for your own sake, wade cautiously. The rocks and stones in these streams are slippery; safe footing often gives way suddenly to unsafe footing, and a tumble can be wet and painful, sometimes dangerous.

There is one problem which I find particularly difficult. If you approach a small pool from below, it is very hard not to frighten any small trout which may be lying in the shallows at the very tail of the pool. To your dismay you then see their bow-waves as they dash upstream to disturb other and better fish, just where you hoped to rise one or two. You may then have to wait at least twenty minutes for the pool to settle down again.

One answer to this is to be prepared to wait. Sometimes, however, I think it is worth approaching a pool at right angles, rather than from below, and putting in to the bank about halfway down the pool, thus avoiding the tail altogether. It's a gambit that can work well. The only remaining answer is simply to trust that the problem won't crop up too often.

To strike successfully on a West Country stream, when a trout takes your fly, you must be alert. You must be constantly alert. If a rise catches you by surprise, or occurs when you happen to be admiring the beauty of the countryside, you will probably hesitate and miss your chance. The trout are quick, very quick, especially in fast water. This does not mean that you should snatch at them, however. A snatch usually results in either a miss or a break. 'Tighten' is a far better word than 'strike'. Tighten deliberately then, without any violence, but do so as soon as you see the rise.

You can fish in either of two ways. Whenever a fair number of trout appear to be rising, you can concentrate on these feeding fish. Or you can fish the water. That is to say, you can float your fly over all the places where you think a trout may be waiting to take an insect on the surface. And you can have a very good day. One of the joys of dry fly fishing on these streams is that your sport is not confined to the days or periods when flies hatch in quantity. At other times as well, trout will often lie high in the water hoping for a stray insect. Food is comparatively scarce, so that they cannot afford to let any good morsel pass them by. They are frequently on the *qui-vive*, even though you may not see them rise.

It is at these times that you need the ability to read a stream, which simply means being able to make good guesses as to where the trout will be ready to take your fly. Without this ability you will certainly waste more casts than you need. It is not difficult. It merely involves trying to put yourself in the place of the trout. If you were a trout with a comparatively empty belly, where would you lie? Your choice as a trout would probably be governed by these considerations. First and foremost, you would choose a place where the current, acting as a conveyor belt, was likely to bring you plenty of food. Second, you would avoid ultra-fast water in which you had to expend a great deal of energy simply to keep your station. And third, you would feel safest where some sort of cover, probably in the form of a bank or a rock or a tree root, was close at hand. If you forewent any of these considerations, it would be the third.

The set of the current is the most important factor. Whenever water from a fairly broad area upstream is gathered together into a fairly narrow run, the food from a wide surface area will also be gathered there. And that is where trout will wait for it. Always look for places where the current is concentrated. This may be in mid-stream or better still, under one of the banks. Then the trout have nearby cover as well. Another good spot is any place where two or more currents converge.

The pace of the current also plays its part. When food is scarce trout are unlikely to wait for it in very slow, slack water. The conveyor belt is too slow for them. Equally, it is too slow for the fisherman and his artificial, since to cover any worthwhile area of water takes ages. When there is a reasonable hatch of fly, or perhaps a reasonable fall of insects from above, then indeed you will see fish rising in the slow water. And they will be worth fishing for too, because you will be fishing the rise and casting only to spots which you can see to be inhabited. When you are fishing the water, however, do not waste time on those slow, still stretches. At the other end of the scale, the current can be too fast for trout. Even if such a current does carry plenty of food, they have to swim too hard simply to stay in position. So they often choose medium-paced water. Or, alternatively, they may find lies close to fast water but protected from it, places from which they can dart out to capture a morsel of food and to which they then return. Places like this occur at the ripply edges of swift currents, also behind rocks and, perhaps less obviously, in front of rocks, where there is always a cushion of comparatively quiet water.

Searching these likely places, while you are fishing the water, is always a tense and exciting business. You never know when a trout's nose will suddenly appear or when your fly will suddenly disappear. So you have to be continually on the look-out, continually ready to take advantage of a rise; perhaps an unexpected rise. And when your judgement of a good lie for a trout turns out to be correct, you have every right to feel a warm glow of self-satisfaction.

You can fish throughout the whole lovely, livelong day. When the trout are rising, you will fish the rise. When they are not, you will fish the water or, if you prefer, switch over to wet fly. With that much time at your disposal you can relax and be unhurried. You can take time off to eat your sandwiches, or simply to enjoy your surroundings, without feeling that you are wasting the few precious minutes when you will catch fish. And, from early June onwards, there may be a good evening rise to round off your day in spectacular style.

Your only fear will be too much rain and consequently too much colour in the water. Showers or drizzle are nothing to worry about. But prolonged and heavy rain will fairly quickly turn the water brown. In the past, before such things were frowned upon, these were ideal conditions for locals to go and get themselves fine baskets of trout on a worm. But those free and easy days are gone and fly fishing, which attracts no trout in dirty water, has to wait till the rivers clear again.

Even so, there is no need for you to sit indoors twiddling your thumbs. You can always go and fish one of the many good still waters which now exist in the West Country. Or if you prefer to fish a river at almost any cost (as I confess I do) you can try the Dart. The Dart is a delightful river by any standard, running through spectacular, often rocky, scenery, and it has the great advantage of being very resistant to colouration. It takes a tremendous amount of rain to colour the Dart.

With any luck, however, the weather will allow you to fish where you like. And you will have a wide choice. I have spoken mainly of the Lyd and the Carey because I know them and love them, but they are only typical of countless other rivers and streams throughout the West Country. To know them also would be to love them also.

All fishing is good. There is really no such thing as bad fishing. Perhaps curiously, I have never even had a bad dream about fishing. But I have had many a pleasant and enjoyable dream in which I have found myself in lovely fishing situations and lovely fishing country. Sometimes this has been recognisable as chalk-stream country. But just as often, if not more so, it has seemed to be the West Country, with its bright chuckling streams and its brave little trout. And indeed I know of no better place to be, awake or asleep.

WILSON STEPHENS

*

West of Weymouth

ALL ANGLERS soon learn there is nothing more boring than other men's fish. Yet occasionally a particular fish comes unexpectedly into one's life, giving things new perspectives in the manner of an Old Testament prophet, catalysing by its presence a whole complex of issues vastly greater than itself. Thus it was about to be (though we were not to know it) when three men stared gloomily into their gin in the smoking room of the Flyfishers' Club, then located in Whitehall Court. I was one of them.

It was a day in early September but that mellow month was giving us a raw deal. Rain, the heavy, relentless, day-long late summer rain was sweeping down outside, almost hiding the great plane trees of the Embankment Gardens in its grey folds. My companions had plenty about which to stare gloomily, for they were refugees from the Oval, where the lunch interval was clearly destined to last from breakfast until stumps. They had come for solace to their second home.

No others were in the room. September is not much of a month for finding Flyfishers in their Club. Most of them are on the river banks then. Ever mindful of the wants of others, I sought to divert the thoughts of my companions from the scurviness of fate in facilitating the escape of the undeserving Australians. For want of a better distraction, I outlined my plan for the following week. It was to be spent in Devon in pursuit of trout. They listened with concern.

To say they did not respond bullishly would be an understatement. The gloom deepened as they re-examined their gin with morbid intensity. 'There's not a decent trout west of Weymouth' said one. Those were the days before the acme of many an angler's

Above　The Dart in autumn – shallows at Holne Chase.
Below　A place for summer grilse to lie – Anne Voss-Bark on the Tamar.

Above   A pattern of rainbows – stock ponds at Durleigh.
Below   The fast-running Lyn – a typical Exmoor stream.

Above   Evening light on the Taw near the Rising Sun Inn at Umberleigh. *Below*   'West of Weymouth' – a brown trout of the Otter on the Deer Park Hotel water at Honiton.

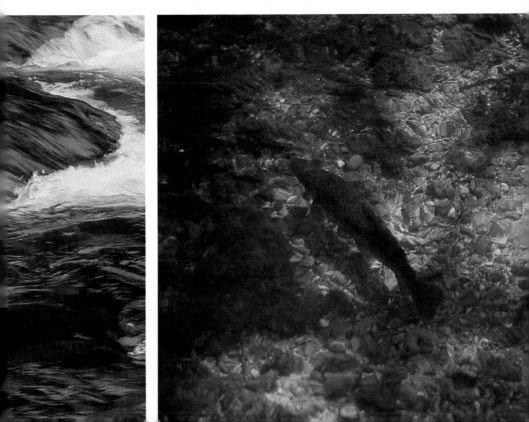

Left　Robin Lemon fishing the evening drift at Blagdon.
Top　Early spring fishing for the wild trout of the Carey.
Centre　Moorland silver – the West Dart above
Hexworthy. *Bottom*　A summer run – the Willow Pool
of the Tamar on the Arundell Arms water below Polson
Bridge.

Above The Yellow Torrish is a favourite fly in cloudy water...
Below ...and takes a fresh-run 12lb Tamar salmon with sea
lice still on the tail. *Right* A sink-tip line for the salmon of the
Exe – John Ruscoe on the Carnarvon Arms Hotel water at Cove.

Above   Wet fly fishing – a deadly method on the fast run-in to a moorland pool. *Below*   A long, wide stretch of the Torridge – Group Captain Norton-Smith fishing Dead Man's Pool.

ambition was to mobilise the financial clout to get to a stillwater stocked with 18-pounders (preferably inexperienced). A decent trout meant a pound and a half.

'There's peal, but you don't get 'em till midnight' offered the other, seeking to strike a cheerful note. 'What will you do in daylight?' River banks in Devon were no place for a sane man with brownies on his mind, it seemed. They sought diligently to dissuade me.

The first speaker recalled catching a half-pounder from the Cherry Brook; but that was a longish time ago, things had probably gone off a bit since then, as they had everywhere. His friend had heard rumours, which he personally discounted, of trout every bit as big as herrings in the Avon, that westernmost of all Avons which rises on Dartmoor and hugs its secrets tight until it reaches the sea at Bigbury Bay. They had naught for my comfort except a replenished glass. They could see no sense in the idea. No more could I. But for those who do only what they see sense in, the unexpected seldom happens. Besides, the theory of 'not a decent trout west of Weymouth' might just conceivably be wrong. And my own theory, that the pleasantest of surprises are likely to be found in surroundings unfrequented by others might just conceivably be right. To go where the rest do not, analogous to that simple formula for riches on the Stock Exchange of buying on a falling market, had led me to some careful exercises in recollection.

Never had I encountered a man who had reported fishing the Otter upstream of the A30 road. From Teign and Dart, Exe and Tamar, the myriad streams of Dartmoor, the northbound combes of Torridge and Taw had come stories of triumph and disaster, of paradise and perfidy, of that whole gamut of elation and disappointment which constitute a fisherman's life. Yet the Otter, the first Devonian river to be crossed by infiltrators from the east, appeared to be unknown for half its length.

Some informants had broken their journeys either to or from the salmon of the far west, and at an hotel on its banks had enjoyed better sport than they had expected. 'Devon brownies' (they spoke the words with the affection reserved for the small unpretentious things of life) had there taken on a new meaning. Some others, mostly well-stricken with years, had penetrated a few miles upstream from Budleigh Salterton towards Ottery St Mary with variable results. Yet that healthy curiosity which differentiates men from apes, by which all human progress has been motivated, which compelled Columbus to sail across the Atlantic and the Vikings to take the swan's path, seemed to have caused none to turn their eyes upstream from Fenny Bridges. And there is as much of the Otter above that point as below it.

In fact a certain difficulty deters the motorist who wishes to spin his steering wheel decisively rightwards and explore those upper reaches. There is no road. Pioneering instincts are called for, and the use of the legs much in demand, as I was to find three days later when my plan was put into effect. I discovered that the real way to this small lost world is by back-tracking for four miles up the A30 to a point beyond Honiton where a lane leads away in fair proximity to the river almost to its source on the high scarp which, a little further on, looks down on Taunton Deane.

The hills are close-knit and secretive, little changed amid all the alterations of post-war England. They are not high, but steep, and convoluted and far from lonely. I found two villages and two hamlets in a dozen miles. They were inhabited by people who believed in guarding their peace and in keeping their eyes open. Nature crowded in closely to the compact family farms. On two steep slopes cataracts of soil, light-hued in undergrowth, marked badger setts. Hounds should do well hereabouts: as the psalmist sang, the little hills would be refuge for foxes, and every man would know their coming and going. This was countryside where, then, light industry had not brought the touch of town.

It took a whole day, measured to late evening, to find a farmer who would let me fish from his fields. Two games of bar billiards and much cider sweetened my approach, so my first sight of the water showed stars reflected in it, dancing and changing shape as the river hurried by, heading for its lengths beyond the high road where, so they said, bigger fish were put in every spring.

Next morning the scene was very different. The narrow valley widened for a stretch at this point. The farmer's arable land, thirty acres or so, lay beyond the far bank. A girder bridge, based on ancient stone pediments, took the tractors and implements to and fro across the stream. Two hundred yards upstream the steep hillside came down to the near-bank, heather and bracken giving place to bramble which grew above the water. There was neither foothold nor casting space there so each day I crossed the bridge and fished from the fields. The next mile up, they said, was mine if I wanted it, and I would have some fish.

The river was brook-size here, with a brook's many changes of pace. In places it chortled merrily along; in others there were respectable pools. Deep runs over stones were interspersed with shallows where the weed growth was enough to provide reason-able hatches of fly. For two days it gave me good sport with enough breakfast-sizers to meet the needs of the family at the farm, and some to take home to the friends with whom I stayed. But there was nothing yet to unship the camera in refutation of the theory that no decent trout rose west of Weymouth.

My estimate of the country had been correct. Buzzards mewed, which is a good accompaniment for fishermen until a better is heard, as it was when a curlew bubbled beyond the high ground across the stream. Once I heard the open-flute call of a ring ouzel, but did not see him; twice the white rump of a dipper went speeding upstream. So too, a little later, did the azure and scarlet jewel of a kingfisher. In these small ways the unexpected was happening, as I hoped it would.

Hence I was not surprised when, on the sun-baked afternoon of the third day, scuffling amid the brambles over the water indicated I was not alone. The field from which I fished was barley stubble. The straw had been baled and now the farmer and his two sons were methodically crossing and recrossing the field with tractor and buckboard, gathering the bales. The clatter of the tractor made concentration on the scuffling difficult; and concentration on the scuffling interrupted my attention to what was going on in the stream ahead of me.

There is scuffling and scuffling and this sort did not seem to be the sort caused by a bird. Nor was it. Eventually, with much peering and leaning, I had a view of the scuffler. Wonder of wonders, a polecat, the first I had seen in England (my only other sighting had been in Wales). Momentarily I had suspected a ferret but the polecat's civilised version is a sleek refined creature compared with the coarse-coated, rough and villainous character which confronted me and, typically, showed no fear. If anything proved the changelessness of this forgotten valley, the polecat did.

Eventually it scuffled off. Almost as an anti-climax I cast a pheasant-tail to the lowest of a series of rise-rings in a little run which swept round a bluff in the bank, my side, upstream. After floating down a foot or two it dimpled under, as pheasant tails had been doing for two days. By reflex action the line tightened solidly.

Very solidly. This was not going to be the pleasant but routine exercise of playing another breakfast-sizer into the net. Could something else unexpected be happening, and salmon lay up here to spawn? Whatever it was came suddenly downstream turning when my silhouette towered over it and my small rod had hooped nearly full circle. Then the reel screamed, the surface exploded in spray and suddenly the tractor's clatter stopped. On the bank came a thumping of gum-boots. One of the farmer's sons was shouting 'It's the big 'un; he's got the big 'un!' Then there were three large men all giving me advice.

'Give me the net', commanded the farmer, 'I'll lift the big sod out.'

And so, in due course, he did. It had been a tense battle in the confined space of the stream before we looked at what proved to be 4 lb 14 oz of noble brown trout, then and still my biggest ever from a stream, seemingly in the prime of life with nothing of the kipeyness of old age about him.

'Never thought to see him out', said one of the sons.

'Gentleman from London comes every month or so to try and catch him', said his father. 'He'll be disappointed now.'

The priest was in my hand. 'Do I knock him out or does he go back?' I asked. 'No, he don't go back', replied the farmer positively. 'You caught him, he's yours, you dunt him; make room for another to grow as big'.

So it was done. And the big fish was to lie in state for an hour or two in the inn where we had met. The evening's drinking cost the regulars less than usual that evening, and me more. A celebratory bottle of whisky changed hands and the trout returned to the farmhouse to be dined off next evening—cold with salad, the farmer's wife predicted.

I have never cast another fly on the upper Otter; nor indeed, on the lower Otter. To have done so then would have been an anti-climax. Soon afterwards I married and in the reorientation which follows so great an event I have never passed that way again. But the big trout remains in my memory as more than a triumph I did not wholly deserve (for though I caught him I had not previously seen and stalked him) but rather as a landmark.

He was the culmination of my decision to circumvent the Thames and all that therein flowed. They represented, in all their wealth of opportunity, Abanar and Pharpar, the Biblical rivers of the south—the obvious and conventional answer to the basic question, in this case the angler's everlasting, 'where?' The gambler's answer, of trying somewhere new in defiance of men's doubts, came off in this case. It proved, moreover, that there was indeed at that time a decent trout west of Weymouth. Perhaps there is another by now.

*

The Wet Fly

THE WET FLY, without any doubt, is the most flexible way of fishing of them all, upstream or down, fast or slow, deep or shallow, in every kind of water. Indeed I do believe that if trout cannot be taken on a correctly presented wet fly then the angler is very unlikely to do much better with the dry. However, there are times when one method may be more productive than the other so the wet fly and the dry must be thought of as complementary. I fish both, depending on conditions or how I happen to be feeling, but generally I think of the wet fly, particularly fished upstream, as the most effective means of filling the bag, mainly because of the rapid rate at which it is possible to cover the water. Dry fly I generally think of as a more leisurely pastime, whereby each pool occupies me for ten minutes rather than two, and each fish taken calls for a pause for thought and a drying of the fly.

Let us consider the trout, that handsomely spotted gentleman of the stream. What does he think of the wet fly? Of course we cannot really answer that question correctly until he can tell us, we can only guess. Trout feed mostly below water, taking in almost any eatable creature they can. The vast family of aquatic flies are taken at all stages of development—as nymphs among the weeds and rocks, as nymphs struggling to the surface before hatching, as the hatched fly on the surface, and then again as the mature spinner returning to lay her eggs and die. On rough streams duns and spinners, especially the latter, often become drowned in the turbulence and are taken below the surface as well as above. I am sure that many trout taken on the wet fly were fooled into thinking that the fly they were taking was just another drowned fly being swirled along in the current.

Snails are also taken, but since they spend most of their time attached to underwater objects, their imitation need not worry the wet fly man unduly. Freshwater shrimps, good old *gammarus pulex*, are a popular food and here is excellent scope for imitation. Shrimps can swim quite strongly, normally only for short distances between cover, but they can be imitated both in fly pattern and behaviour and are a very useful addition to the fly box. Small fish are taken by the trout, indeed it is an exception to find a keepable trout without a fish of some sort in its stomach. Bullheads and minnows are the most popular but loach and baby trout and salmon will also be found. The fry of dace and grayling where they occur are also taken so we can see that small fish form a substantial part of the trout's diet. A fish may take a hundred nymphs but will get just as much nourishment from one nice minnow. I am sure that the faster-moving wet fly is often taken in mistake for a fish. It is common to take quite a small trout, less than 8 inches long, while fishing after dark for sea trout. One night last summer I caught a grayling of nearly 2 lb on a long-shank size 6 lure while sea trouting. Food for thought for the tiny-fly school!

Fishing our wet fly upstream is at once the most effective and the most difficult method. By fishing upstream, which also means up and across, sometimes directly across, the angler is more or less behind the fish and therefore less likely to be seen. Trout have remarkably good vision all around them, except directly behind, so great caution is required at all times. The fish straight upstream of you may be unalarmed but his small brother near you will shoot upstream if he sees you, spreading panic as he goes. Remember that in most of our West Country rivers you are dealing with totally wild trout to whom any shadow or movement spells danger. I find many anglers fail to catch trout not because their casting or fishing technique is at fault but because their approach to the river bank is so noisy and blatant. By the time they get a fly in the water any decent trout in the vicinity will have fled to the shelter of the tree roots. Success comes to the man who moves like a hunter stalking a deer: no thumps on the bank, no shadows over the water, no splash of waders or of line. You must respect the trout for what he is, a wild creature in his own environment.

For all my trouting I now use a 9 foot carbon rod, a number 5 line and a long leader. I like a longish rod because I find it makes roll casting and general line control much easier. Many anglers prefer rods much shorter, right down to 6 feet 10 inches or so, but I stick to the 9-footer even on the small streams. I do occasionally find myself attached to thorn bushes and nettles but no more than most and it is a fine lesson in patience. I like a long leader, normally 10 to 12 feet because this puts that thick old fly line well away from the fish, making the inevitable disturbance it causes less obvious. In high summer, with rivers very low and clear, I often use a leader up to 14 feet long. I taper these down from a thick butt of say 16 lb breaking strain in easy stages to a 3 foot point of 2½ lb.

For upstream fishing, indeed for any wet fly fishing, I find no need for a vast selection of patterns. The number one wet fly in my box is the Coachman. It certainly bears no resemblance to any insect I know but it is one of the most consistently successful flies I have ever used. Size is important. Use a size 12 in early spring, reducing to a 14 as the water warms and clears in summer, and down to a 16 in very low water. This quick guide to size can be applied to all standard wet flies on our rivers. Other successful patterns are the Black Spider, Greenwell's Glory and the Pheasant Tail with either a ginger, badger or blue dun hackle.

I have a dressing of my own which I often use. It has no name but has caught me hundreds of trout since I first tied it some thirteen years ago. It is a simple hackled fly, with a blue dun hackle and tail and a body of dark olive seal's fur ribbed with fine gold wire. Call it Pilk's Favourite if you like. It is one I always carry in my box.

Armed with the right tackle how do we go about catching trout on our upstream wet fly? I consider one of the most important factors is the speed at which you cover the water. Given a beat of say three-quarters of a mile on a smallish river, to fish it correctly you should cover the whole beat comfortably in a day's fishing, and by the whole beat I do not mean every inch of water. There are many places not worth covering, others where it may pay you to linger awhile. On the small streams you will only find your decent trout in the pools. The runs in between are generally too fast and shallow to hold fish of any size and should be ignored. Each pool should first be approached very carefully, usually by wading up from the run below. Wading is absolutely essential if you are to cover the water properly since it keeps the angler low on the skyline. If you are a right-handed caster it will be easier to cover the water from the right bank (that is the left bank facing upstream) but if you only have left-bank fishing then backhand casting will be necessary except on the wider and more open reaches.

Good trout will often lie well back in the tail of the pools and they can very easily be frightened. Normally the best fish will lie close to the bank so put your fly up along your own bank first, then fan your casts across to the other side. The fly and the leader must sink readily. Spit on your fly and allow it and the leader to trail in the water behind you before starting to fish. This should make everything sink nicely. If you prefer it, use one of the sink-mix potions that are now available. Floating nylon throws a terrible shadow and can scare every fish within yards. So, your first cast is a fairly short one, say no more than a rod length of fly line out from the tip ring close to the bank upstream of you. Give the fly a second or two to sink then retrieve your line as it drifts towards you. With a short line this is best accomplished by raising the rod tip rather than stripping in by hand which is where I find the longish rod handy. Before the current drags your fly into the rough water lift off and cast again. Put the next cast a foot or two out from the bank and gradually place each successive cast further and further across until you are within inches of the other bank. At all times keep your eyes glued to where you think your fly is and try to retrieve slack line just a little bit faster than the current so you are always in contact with your fly.

When a fish takes, a number of things may happen. Firstly, if your fly is close to the surface, which is usually the case, you may see a proper rise-form as the fish turns down with the fly. You may actually see the fish itself as it takes. You may not see anything at all except that the tip of the line, drifting down with the flow, may stop or jerk. You may feel a pull. At any of these signs, strike, but not fiercely, just raise your rod smoothly and with any luck the trout may be on. If a fish comes to your fly and does not get hooked he is worth another cast providing he has not been pricked. A trout which has felt the hook will certainly not come again unless he is very small and foolish. If the trout has missed the fly, or refused, try him once again and then move on. This is where so many anglers waste so much time. They will keep flogging at a fish which has long since lost all interest and will even stay there changing flies. Far, far better to move on, perhaps coming back to him later when he may be feeding again with confidence.

Move slowly on up the pool, covering all the likely water, but pay particular attention to the water under the banks, along any large rocks or fallen trees, and into any eddy. The best fish always lie where they can get the maximum amount of food in maximum security with the minimum of effort. Work these factors out for yourself as you move up the pool. Anywhere where the current narrows the stream of waterborne food becomes concentrated. If there is an eddy right beside the main flow with trees overhanging the water and roots along the bank then here you have the classic place for the grand-daddy of the pool. On the larger rivers these likely lies will be much less apparent so they need to be covered very systematically except for the very fast shallows where you will normally catch only salmon parr.

To my mind the very essence of the upstream wet fly is the recovery of the slack line and the ability to keep in touch with the fly. There is often not a direct sense of touch at all, only a very real sixth sense, which comes with practice, telling you when there is a take. I often find myself tightening into a fish without being conscious why I have done so. This can be explained, up to a point, by the fact that a taking fish can often be anticipated in a precise location and by tightening when the fly is just at that spot a fish will be found to be on. However, I catch fish in too many widely ranging places for this explanation and I can only put it down to the subconscious mind reacting to stimuli of which the conscious mind is unaware. Concentration, of course, is vital. Try to be aware at all times of exactly where your fly is and what it is doing. I can guarantee that if you take your eyes off the water for a second, to watch a kingfisher coming past or an old heron beating heavily upriver, that will be just the moment when a fish takes you and by the time you can do anything about it he will have ejected the fly. It is all part of the fun of fishing; for if you never take time to watch the birds and the beasts of the river bank your day will be sadly impoverished at a greater cost than the loss of the odd fish.

When trout are lying near the surface and can be seen rising then the ordinary unweighted flies which rarely sink more than a few inches will catch all the trout you ever want. However, during high summer, particularly during the heat of the day, there is often scope for a weighted fly or nymph. Nymphing in our West Country spate rivers differs dramatically from the more publicised nymphing of the chalk streams. The chalk stream man casts to a fish he can see and in some cases he can watch the take. The late Frank Sawyer claimed often to see the nymph itself in the water and the white inside of the trout's mouth in the water as it opened to take it. Very seldom is it possible to imagine doing anything like this on a spate river where the water even when low and clear often carries a tinge of colour. Sometimes this is due to cattle upstream but more often because of the very fine silt the water carries in suspension. The chalk stream, remember, is filtered at its source by mother nature.

So, if trout and nymph are both invisible, what can we look for as indication of a take? The answer is the point where the leader penetrates the surface of the water. I like a nice long fine leader, the butt greased to within three or four feet of the fly, down in fact to the last knot. This allows the nymph to sink so far but then remain at a fairly constant depth as it comes downstream. I use a fairly big nymph, about size 12, and find this is more effective than small sizes. The standard Pheasant Tail, well weighted, is probably the only one you will need, although an olive-type nymph or a Sawyer Killer Bug will also be taken readily; but as with all fly fishing I consider the pattern to be less important than the manner in which it is used.

The type of water offering the best chance with the nymph is the slow deep pool. Cast your nymph carefully upstream, let it sink, and keep your eyes to the magic point where the nylon goes through the surface. This may twitch, sometimes sharply, sometimes imperceptibly, or else the nylon may stop dead, as though the nymph has snagged the bottom, but on any of these signs strike instantly. As with the upstream wet fly, slack line must be recovered as it drifts towards you but not so fast that the tip of the line itself is actually pulled. With a greased leader this would cause a very obvious ripple on the surface, enough to scare your fish.

Nymphing is primarily a technique for the hot still days of July and August when the very river itself seems lifeless. The rough and tumbly water of the high moorland rivers is not really suitable, although the larger pools may offer a chance, and it is not really of much use on a windy day when there is a big ripple. However, when things are right the nymph can often yield a good bag of fish when all else has failed. If the nymph is not taken on the drift try the induced take. The chalk stream man may wonder how one can induce a trout to take which you cannot see and cannot locate.

Well, in most pools, the trout population is sufficiently high for your nymph to be seen by several fish, especially when it is in a good place, such as in the deeper water along the undercut banks. Try an ordinary drift first and then cast again and when the nymph has finished sinking lift the rod point very gently, bringing the nymph towards the surface as the real nymph does when it is rising to hatch. Do not lift too fast and cause line wake on the surface. Nymphing needs keen eyesight and a good deal of concentration but it is a fascinating form of fly fishing and one which can produce quality fish in adverse conditions.

Harking back to what I said earlier about where to find the better-sized trout I spent a very enjoyable time hunting these 'Charlies' on the higher Tamar last summer. Each pool always has one particular place where the best fish can be expected and as I worked my way up the beat I selected the most likely spots and fished them carefully. I took one or two respectable trout in the 6 to 8 oz bracket, plus several smaller ones which went back, and then came to a very large pool on a bend where a small ditch joined the river on the far bank. The mouth of this ditch opened out into the pool just at the point where the flow from the neck had steadied to a nice comfortable pace for holding trout, and there was a quiet eddy, well overhung with brambles and cow parsley. Within this little haven a good trout was occasionally rising, sometimes on the edge of the current or well up towards the ditch.

To reach that fish I needed to cast a long line of some 15 or 16 yards—chicken feed to a reservoir man with plenty of room all round but not easy with the 7 foot brook rod I was using that day with a tangle of branches close behind me. The back cast had to be aimed at a narrow alleyway between the branches and the last few yards of line had to be shot each time to reach the fish. After several attempts, during which I caught three different species of deciduous tree behind me, I put the fly just beyond the current into the eddy. No response. My trout must have been well up the ditch. Several deciduous trees later, the fly fell right again. This time a take and a 6 inch brownie skittered across the pool towards me. I shook him off and tried again. More excursions into the vegetation. Then the fly dropped with a plonk into the middle of the eddy. The sudden appearance of a small Coachman just behind his left gill cover was too much for the trout. He turned back on it savagely and I saw the water heave. The rod tip went up and was pulled sharply down. The trout, fortunately, headed out into the pool and not up the ditch. He played well, leaping twice before coming to the net, and I lifted out a fine ¾-pounder. Not a big trout, not even keepable in some parts of the country, but a fine wild-bred brownie, one I felt I had well and truly earned!

Now let me tell you something. Fishing the wet fly downstream is often regarded as a duffer's pastime. You chuck a fly across the stream and let the current do the rest. True, in some places that is all you need to do, but it would be a dull world if that was all there was. Beginners should start off with the downstream wet fly because it gives the indifferent caster a chance of a few fish and helps to boost confidence. It also gives a good grounding in rivercraft, wading, line control and the practical application of overhead, side and roll casting. It can be used on any water but is at its best on wider rivers and on streamy water rather than on the pools. If there are no fish rising it makes sense to fish downstream and cover a large area of water fairly quickly. Early in the season, when feeding fish are scarce, this will give you an excellent chance.

Flies for the downstream fishing can be a little larger and brighter than for upstream. The Coachman is always good and so is the Black Spider. A fly with a little silver or gold in it, such as a Butcher or a Wickham, can be very effective and I am sure these flasher patterns are taken for small fish. What else can face the current in the manner that the downstream wet fly does?

Starting at the neck of the pool, or the head of a nice streamy run, put a short line down and across the river at an angle of about 45 degrees to your own bank. Let the current swing this around until the line lies directly below you, lift off and cast again. In very fast water do not cast too much across the stream or the fly will whip round too quickly, skating on the surface. On slower water gently pull in line as the fly swings round in order to keep in contact with your fly, and to give it more 'life'. Follow the line round with your rod tip which also helps to keep you in touch with your fly. I like to hold the rod low, the tip almost touching the water, because this way I can feel a fish at once. Fishing downstream you are fishing 90 per cent of the time by feel, indeed that is how we fish for sea trout in complete darkness. A take will be felt as a distinct pull and all you need to do is tighten gently. Many trout, particularly in fast water, will hook themselves. Many others will just as easily fail to get hooked and I reckon you must accept that you will be lucky to land a third of the fish that come to your fly. The reason for this is that the trout is looking straight at you and the fly tends to be pulled clean out of its mouth. Enough fish will be hooked, however, to make it worthwhile, particularly if you keep moving and covering fresh water. A cast and a step is a good maxim. Make your cast, let it fish round, and as you lift off to cast again take one step downstream.

In very productive water where one cast will cover several different likely lies it obviously pays to fish more slowly though one should keep moving steadiy. Having taken a fish the beginner will often cast into the same water again and again hoping for a repeat performance which, sadly, is most unlikely. He should move on a pace and recast, working steadily downstream. It pays to cast a fairly long line but only when the water close in has been covered with a short line. Extend line, a yard each cast, until either you are reaching the far bank or else are casting as far as you can with comfort. Then start to move down.

Wading, particularly on wide rivers, is pretty well essential, and you may be surprised how little the wading angler disturbs the fish, especially if he wades deep and slowly. I have caught trout within a few yards of my boots on many occasions. The essential thing is not to stir up great clouds of mud from the bottom, not to splash about like a wallowing elephant, and not send heavy ripples across the pool. You must move slowly and stealthily.

When wading you will need to deal with your trout from the position you are in, out in the river, so all your gear must be carried on your back. I have a folding net on my bag and having netted a fish find that I need three hands, one to hold the net, one for the trout and one for the rod. Sometimes I have been convulsed with laughter to see the antics of people trying to deal with this situation. The solution is simple—push the butt end of your rod down the top of your waders and you have sufficient hands for the net and the fish. A word of warning. If your trout is worth keeping, kill him while he is still on the hook and in the net. If you drop a lively trout in any depth of water he will be gone in a flash.

I learned a poignant lesson last year when I was wading and fishing a stretch of water over a hundred yards long. I killed seven trout, two of them quite good fish, and placed them in my landing net while I fished on. When I eventually climbed out of the water I had lost three of them through a hole in the meshes, inevitably two of those being the best fish. I searched the river bottom very carefully but nary a fin did I find.

I mentioned earlier how wet and dry fly were complementary techniques and I recall a day on the Tamar during the awful drought of 1976 when the wet fly proved to be the better of the two. It was a Bank Holiday Monday at the end of May and the drought, though well established, was not yet at its worst. A few fields of hay had already been cut and the general feeling among farmers was that this was bound to mean rain. I set out intending to enjoy myself with the dry fly. Trout were rising well and a variety of ephemerids and terrestrials were on the water. However, after a very few casts it was apparent that I would require the patience of Job. My fly sat motionless on the surface. The flow of the river was already so reduced the pool was virtually static. There was my fly, proudly stationary, a yard above the rising trout.

Well, since the fish would not go to the fly then I reasoned that the fly must go to the fish. Off came the dry fly and on went two small wet flies, a Coachman on the dropper and a Pilk's Favourite on the point. I fished this time as a stillwater man would—a cast, allow them to sink, then the retrieve. The results were immediate and startling. As the flies combed the dead water of the pools trout popped out from beneath rock ledges and alongside clay banks to engulf them with great gusto. I had some truly wonderful sport.

The high spot of the afternoon was a deep pool with a small feeder stream on the opposite bank and from the bay at the mouth of this stream I took four keepable fish without moving my feet, the best being a veritable monster of 15 ounces. I killed ten trout in all and decided that was enough. I laid the fish on the grass beneath a great oak tree, the 15-ouncer at the top and a precocious eight-and-a-bit incher at the bottom, and the remaining eight fish were like peas in a pod. There was not half an inch variation in length, nor half an ounce in weight between the lot of them. They were all as near as dammit 10 inch half-pound trout in absolutely tip-top condition.

The Coachman and his sombre companion of the leader were looking a little the worse for wear by now. So, perhaps, was I, as I started the long treck back through the meadows with the sun still blistering down and a cloud of midges dancing in the haze beneath the oak.

THE BLUE UPRIGHT

The West Country dressing of the Blue Upright . . . is the wet fly fisherman's dry fly, meant to be fished on the top of the water. The body, often of quill, and the hackles of stiff cock, prevent it from becoming water-logged . . . and it is designed to be fished in narrow rough waters, very much upstream, with a short line and frequent casts.

T.C. KINGSMILL MOORE, 1960.

Here [on the Barle] *with a little aluminium box in your pocket or a few flies stuck in your coat lapel you will fish all day with a cast so fine it looks like the strand of a brunette's hair . . . and the flies will be small hackled Blue Upright, with most of its hackle snipped off; the Hare's Ear, Pheasant Tail, Greenwell's Glory and, as the season gets on, the apparently irresistable little Tup.*

NEGLEY FARSON, 1942.

You should also have ready the Hare's Fleck, generally called the Blue Upright in Devonshire, and strongly recommended by all fishing books; but, and I know it is rank heresy to say so, I don't care for it one bit, and I am supported in this dislike by William Bale, the Lynmouth shoemaker.

CLAUDE F. WADE, 1903.

MARCUS ERVINE-ANDREWS

✣

Bodmin Born

DRIVING ALONG the high road, west to Bodmin, just before you get to the Jamaica Inn, you cross a road bridge which looks so much part of the road that you may well miss seeing the flicker of water underneath. It is a tiny stream, little more than a brook, which has just risen a few miles away on High Moor near Brown Willy. It is the river Fowey (pronounced *Foy*), and if you turn off a lane to the left near the inn you can drive for most of the time beside the Fowey south to the Golitha Falls.

Golitha is unusual, even for Cornwall. The river runs through a dark wood, dropping as it goes, running faster and faster, until it smashes against huge boulders in a turmoil of white water and gouged-out pools, rather like the Lyn below Watersmeet, another very bright-water stream. The surroundings of the Fowey here are queerly impressive. Tall trees keep out the sun and almost every branch and bole are covered with long strands of green lichen or moss and as you climb over rocks to follow the river the roots of the trees bar your way like the ribs of half-buried monsters. All around you are rocks, some the size of a house, all in this green half-light of the wood.

When you see Golitha and the run of the river below, on to Lewarne and Lanhydrock, you will realise why the Cornish have a reputation for the worm. The river runs through wooded valleys all the way and the trees are thick on the banks and their branches hang tangled overhead so that only a worm or a small spinner can be got to the lies. However, where the banks have been cleared there is some wonderful fly water which delights your heart even to look at. You generally need advice where to go.

The Fowey is very much a sea trout river and they run large.

They come in early and in March and April I have seen fish up to 13 lb—far bigger than you would get on many other rivers of this size. The school peal of about ¾ lb arrive in June but the big run is at the end of July and August. By mid-August the big fish are out of condition and hardly worth eating. If you catch one then it is best to put it back to spawn.

You can take sea trout on the fly during the day when they are fresh in from the sea. Then they will take almost any fly with plenty of flash that looks like a small fish, such as a Silver Invicta, and towards evening the Invicta may take a salmon as well. Size and presentation are, however, more important than pattern.

For night fishing you have to be careful to make sure your pool is free of snags if you are going to fish with more than one fly on your cast and in any case your point must be nylon of at least 8–10 lb breaking strain. If you hear school peal skittering or see their arrowheads in the water at the tail of the pool then most will be travelling fish, but some will remain to explore the pool, and these take your fly so fiercely that unless you are very careful you may be broken. You need what we call 'good fingers'.

But the old residents of the pool are quite different. They often lie just near the surface and suck in your fly so gently you feel you may have hooked a leaf or a piece of grass. If they feel any pressure they let go at once so that people say 'they're coming short tonight'. To hook these fish best I prefer to fish upstream so that the fly is pulled into their mouth and the flex of the rod softens their first explosion of anger. If you fish downstream with the rod pointing at the fly the trout will feel the tight line at once and eject and if it does not the rod cannot flex to soften the take.

In high summer there is often a pressure of anglers for the sea trout and for sheer enjoyment of being on your own there is nothing better than to go up to the moors with a light fly rod and a gossamer cast. The wild brown trout are small but as intelligent and as difficult to take as any on the chalk streams.

The Fowey goes out to the sea on the south coast, in the long and lovely estuary of the town of the same name, the ancient seaport of Fowey which sent ships to the Crusades.

The sister river of the Fowey is the Camel, which is very like it, very clear, fast flowing, and rises not far away on the same moors, and is almost the same length—about 25 miles—but the Camel flows south before turning to the north and the long estuary at

Padstow, the little fishing port on the north coast which is said to have taken its name from St Petroc who came from Ireland to convert the Cornish to Christianity. Cornwall is full of the memories of saints, as you can tell from the names of so many of the villages.

The Camel is not really of much interest to fishermen above Camelford but reaches its main status as a river a few miles further on by Trecarne and from here down to the tide there are about 150 pools where salmon and sea trout lie. On the whole the Camel is better for salmon than the Fowey but not so good for the sea trout. It is a very beautiful river and winds its way through a wooded valley through two great spurs of the moor that cut you off completely from the outside world. The old stone bridges that cross the river are fascinating, made of huge mellowed granite blocks that you imagine are so old they might have been cut by stonemasons at the time of King Arthur.

There is a good run of sea trout but the great attraction of the Camel are the winter salmon which lie in pools of anything from 3 to 15 feet deep. There are always a few spring or summer salmon and grilse to be had but the main run of heavy grilse is in October, November and December, with a few salmon in the 17–25 lb category. These winter fish on both the Fowey and Camel average about 11 lb, made up of the occasional 20-pounder and a fair percentage of fish in the 4–7 lb range. You will also get the occasional winter fish that goes over 30 lb. Pretty good even on a big river and for small streams like this really remarkable.

ROBIN LEMON

*

Lake Fishing

THE WEST COUNTRY has many beautiful lakes. Some, like Dozmary, which is said to hold King Arthur's sword, have a romantic and legendary aura about them as well, but for the fly fisherman the one lake he thinks of first is Blagdon. It was on this lovely sheet of water, in its fertile valley of the Mendips just south of Bristol, that the most spectacular trout fishing ever known in England was recorded.

When Blagdon was opened in 1904 the average weight of trout taken was between 3½ and 4½ lb. In 1905 *The Field* of 6 May reported that two anglers, Mr M.R.L. White and Mr R.C. Hardy Corfe, fishing the March Brown, took twenty trout in one day with a total weight of 91½ lb. The largest weighed 8 lb 4 oz. These remarkable results were partly due to the rich feeding in this newly flooded valley but also to the lack of fishing pressure. In the early days you could get a permit only through knowing a director of Bristol Waterworks. It was very little fished and the trout grew large. The average weight began to decline in later years but even today, with considerable fishing pressure, Blagdon and Chew produce trout of an average of around 2 lb and the first run of a Mendip rainbow still has to be felt to be believed.

It was also at Blagdon that the first imitative patterns of lake insects, close copies of the larvae and pupae found in the trouts' stomachs, were developed by the local doctor, H.A. Bell (1888–1974), during the 1920s and 1930s. Some of his originals, the Blagdon Buzzer, Amber Nymph and the Grenadier, are in the Flyfishers' Club museum in London.

In the south-west as a whole there is tremendous variety of stillwater fishing. Some of the high moorland reservoirs have been left as natural trout fisheries. The small wild trout breed in the inflowing streams. Fishing is very cheap or in some cases free. Having been mainly a river fisherman with lake fishing taking second place, it was not until Chew Valley Lake opened in 1957 that I began to love both types of fishing almost equally. The charm of wild fish in the rivers can never be surpassed but stillwater fishing is so much more than the chuck-and-chance-it that people used to think it was. It has most exciting and interesting features which test the skill of any fisherman; in some respects—dare I say it?—more than in river fishing.

At Chew in the early years there were abundant fly hatches and fishing imitative patterns brought the best results. Perhaps the hatches are less abundant now but I believe, and so do I think some of the regulars at Chew and Blagdon, that the best of the fishing comes from close observation of aquatic life and the use of patterns to imitate the natural insect—particularly snails, buzzers (midge pupae of various sizes and colours), olives, sedges, damsel nymphs and daddy-long-legs. Lures catch many fish at the beginning and end of the season, especially at Chew with its abundance of coarse fish fry, but right through the season traditional fly and nymph patterns bring the most exciting results.

One April day not long ago, three weeks after the opening of the season, I was fishing the north shore of Blagdon with a friend and whilst others nearby were fishing large lures and having a lean time we each caught eight fish. Of my total bag of 23 lb 10 oz, four rainbows were taken on a Worm Fly and three rainbows and a brown on an Amber Nymph. The next day we had similarly good results, retrieving slowly with a long leader on a floating line. Another day late in May near the dam I caught four magnificent rainbows, the largest of 5 lb 8 oz, in just two hours' fishing with the Amber Nymph. I have had so many examples of success with these imitative patterns.

Of course I have had a few blank days when nothing seems to work, particularly when you get that vicious algal bloom in the water. Always ring up before a visit especially in the summer months to enquire about conditions; but even so there was one day at Chew when there was a heavy algal bloom in the water when my son and I, fishing from a boat, had a limit each on Dunkeld and Polystickle, fished on fast-sinking lines near the underwater pumps close to the dam. No doubt the fish had gathered there because of the increased oxygen level and the greater clarity of water beneath the algae.

From 133 day and evening visits to Blagdon and Chew I have taken 461 fish, not counting those returned, and no less than 105 of those on buzzers and various nymphs, 75 on the Worm Fly, and the majority of the rest on traditional wet fly patterns, chiefly Mallard and Claret and Invicta. Lures have taken a few but they have not been so consistent. As you can imagine, I have a soft spot for those wonderful lakes.

In south Somerset, near Yeovil, is Sutton Bingham, which was like a miniature Chew when it was first opened. Again here I find, in the spring, that imitative patterns do best. In the Quantocks, Clatworthy, though not so fertile as some of the other Somerset reservoirs, has plenty of fly life, and small black flies seem to do best there. The regulars say that a small dark fly should always be kept in the team of flies fished.

On the edge of Exmoor is Wimbleball, a big recently opened reservoir of some 374 acres compared with Clatworthy's 150. The first year's sport was marvellous. Over 27,000 fish were taken in 1980; the largest rainbow, of 6 lb 10 oz, had been grown on in the lake from a stocking of 5 to 6 inch fish. The brown trout are not being taken as well as was hoped, which is something of a mystery, but they may show more when fly life is better established. They could be feeding very deep. Many heavyweights have been seen and will present a great challenge to the anglers in the future.

The best spots I have found at Wimbleball are the shallows of Besson and Ruggs Bay, the large Cow Moor Bay, and the other bays dotted round the lake. My best bag during the season was a limit of five fish, weighing 16 lb 1 oz, the largest a rainbow of 4 lb 12 oz, but others took many better ones. I found the Black and Peacock Spider and the Worm Fly a good bet as many of the fish contained snails. Buzzers, yellow-bodied flies and small nymphs were popular with a lot of anglers.

A friend of mine, fishing the drift at Wimbleball with a team of two traditional patterns on 5 lb breaking strain nylon, was heavily smashed on the take by something big, so it could have been one of those enormous browns. If you are drift fishing—and many anglers like the peace and quiet of the boat—then do remember to take a drogue with you as well as an air cushion. Both, I assure you, are essential to comfortable boat fishing and so are a pair of waterproof trousers as well as a coat.

Now we cross the Exe to the more acid upland reservoirs. In the Dartmoor National Park there is actually free fishing for small wild brown trout at two reservoirs, Avon Dam and Meldon, and sometimes in the summer a quite reasonable catch is possible on small dark flies to a long fine leader. Your reactions on these clear moorland lakes need to be very quick indeed.

Dartmoor has two stocked fisheries, both of them very clear lakes, at Fernworthy near Chagford, and at Kennick, near Bovey Tracy. Kennick and the adjoining Tottiford lake are surrounded by woods and huge colourful rhododendrons and visitors say these are the most beautiful lakes they have ever seen. The 1980 catch of some 13,000 fish shows how popular and prolific they are but I must warn you that in this exceptionally clear water the fish can soon become very wary and several anglers on the bank thrashing the water will soon drive them away. There is good sport with dry fly at hawthorn and sedge times. Small dark patterns of wet flies (sized 14 and 12) generally do best.

To me, however, the most picturesque reservoir in the southwest is Burrator, near Plymouth, because of its unique surroundings of moor and tors and forest. It is a natural brown trout fishery supplemented with surplus fry and token stocks of sizeable rainbows throughout the season. This gin-clear water with its shy fish in these lovely surroundings is a great challenge to visiting anglers from the opaque waters of the Midlands. They should fish very fine on a long leader with patterns that imitate the natural, about which C.F. Walker once wrote:

The fly dresser's aim should be not to try to imitate the natural fly in all its part and colour, which is anyhow impossible, but merely to suggest to the trout that this bunch of fur and feather is in fact an insect of the kind it purports to be: in terms of art, if you like, 'to catch a likeness' rather than to paint a portrait.

Seaside holidaymakers in Devon and Cornwall are sometimes surprised to find very good fly fishing not far away from the coasts. There is the 65 acre lake at Argal, near Penryn, Falmouth, and Porth, of 38 acres, near Newquay. Both are stocked fisheries in attractive surroundings. Then there is Upper Tamar Lake, near

Bude, which was flooded in 1975 and has become a very productive water with plenty of fly life, and Wistlandpound (41 acres) in picturesque country in north Devon. A high moorland lake set in Bodmin Moor, near Liskeard, is Siblyback, of 140 acres.

The lure, nymph and dry fly will all take fish on these reservoirs. However, local anglers, myself included, would put the Black and Peacock Spider high on the list for consistency, together with similar flies like the Black Gnat and Coch-y-Bondhu; these particularly on the less fertile lakes like Siblyback.

I must emphasise that normally the water temperature in these lakes is lower than in lowland reservoirs and this being so it is no good persistently fishing the surface with a floating line on a bitterly cold day early or late in the season. Much better to fish deep and slow with a leaded nymph or even a lure.

Every angler, of course, has his own pet patterns and makes his own discoveries. I am no exception. On a recent visit to the United States of America I discovered the Woolly Worm, a favourite lake pattern in the States. The dressing is as follows: a brown hackle is wound palmer-style down a longshank hook and overtied with chenille, leaving plenty of hackle showing. The chenille should be either green or a rusty brown. Fished slowly, at all depths, the Woolly Worm appears to be most attractive to rainbows and is also effective for browns. Varying sizes, from 14s and 12s to 8s, are advisable as a small pattern will often succeed where a larger one fails. I assume that it represents any type of larvae or pupae, especially of the caddis and damsel flies, the hackle giving it a sparkle of life as it is drawn though the water.

In the last two years my fishing diary shows that the Woolly Worm has accounted for more fish than any other fly in all the stillwaters I have fished. It often pays off when all else fails. John Jones, a very good angler who fishes Upper Tamar regularly, was intrigued by the Woolly Worm and, having used it, now swears by it.

The number of privately owned stillwater fisheries has grown considerably in recent years. Probably the best-known in the West Country is Stafford Moor, a 14 acre lake near Dolton, not far from Torrington, in north Devon. Several smaller lakes are dotted round the region. All provide a fascinating alternative to fishing on the large reservoirs. They generally produce larger fish too, and naturally you have to pay more for a day's fishing.

Even though these small lakes are well stocked it is surprising how quickly the fish become wary; though I suppose it is not all that surprising as they can easily see the angler on the bank, and movement and continuous casting are bound to scare fish. There are also always many pricked fish which will be exceptionally shy; and so often on these small intimate lakes you see anglers using heavy reservoir equipment, thrashing out lines as long as they possibly can with no thought of concealment. They will take the odd gullible fish but to achieve greater success a far more delicate approach is needed: smaller outfits, less casting, more stealth.

I know Stafford Moor best, having fished there regularly since it was first opened in 1973. It was created from a marshy area and is well supplied with water from a number of springs. The water has never been absolutely clear so that this, together with its fairly large size, makes concealment of less importance, though it is a factor which must not be forgotten.

The fishery is scenically attractive and well run. Rainbows and browns are stocked and the average size is around the 2 lb mark with the fish in superb condition. Several heavyweights are always present to add extra thrill and expectation. Brown trout, introduced in recent years, are magnificent fish and there is always the chance of catching one in double figures; and browns of 5–7 lb are not uncommon. The same applies to the rainbows though the largest caught so far was over 14 lb.

Fish are taken at Stafford Moor and at similar small lakes on lures, nymphs, wet and dry flies of all shapes and sizes, and again sometimes the fish are so fussy nothing will tempt them at all. Close observation of the water is needed and an assessment of conditions is essential. You know what to fish if there is a good fall of hawthorns, or if you see olives and buzzers hatching, sedges or gnats. Damsels also feature prominently later in the season. Imitative patterns of whatever is about usually do well. In 1980 there was, I believe, for the first time, a substantial hatch of mayfly and some good sport was had on the artificial, both dry and nymph.

As always in the south-west, small black flies, 12s and 14s, seem to be high on the list of successful flies, and Stafford Moor is no exception. Black and Peacock Spiders and Black Gnats of various kinds account for a large number of fish. Totting up catches from my own fishing diary, out of 368 fish caught at Stafford Moor,

Black and Peacock Spiders, Black Gnats and Black Buzzers accounted for 120. The next most successful was—yes!—the Woolly Worm. In fact I think it was *the* most successful as I only started using it there during the last two years and it has accounted for seventy fish. The dry Hawthorn, Sedge, Invicta, Corixa and Pheasant Tail Nymph figure fairly prominently among other successful patterns as also does a Muddler Minnow fished fast across the surface to make a wake.

Sticking my neck out again, I found another successful lake pattern by accident. On a fairly cold day in the season I had been fishing various lures and flies without touching a fish. Eventually I tied on a Butcher and as I tested the knot the wings pulled off in my hand. I didn't bother to change the fly but trimmed off what remained of the black hackle, leaving just the silver body and the black head. With this, on a floating line, I caught the limit of fish in a very short space of time. I have used this sparse-looking thing several times since with a lot of success and now carry a number tied up like it in my box.

The wingless Butcher fished fast or slow seems to attract fish. I suppose it may represent a nymph, the silver body might suggest transparency, and it could also look like a small fish. Incidentally, I am told that T.C. Ivens created the famous Black and Peacock Spider in a not dissimilar way. He was fishing an Alder without success and decided to clip off the wings. The fly immediately began to take fish!

I must tell you, finally, about my greatest thrill at Stafford Moor one day in June. A few fish were showing on the surface but no particular natural flies could be seen. I cast out a small dry Black Gnat, size 14, on a 4 lb leader. Within a few seconds there was a swirl and the fly disappeared. I tightened and the fish took off like a rocket. Many yards of backing went before the fish turned and leapt, its huge broad flank flashing bright silver. I must say I did have doubts about holding it, especially when it decided to hug the bank to my left, leaving a small promontory with a small tree at the point of it between me and the fish. Stretching the rod out as far as I could over the water to prevent tangling with the tree I eventually managed to get the trout to move out. Even then it wasn't finished. I don't know how long the struggle went on but I know I was exhausted as well as the fish. It was a beautiful hen rainbow of exactly 7 lb. I have had bigger fish there but nothing which gave me quite such a thrill.

So, there you are! I tell you all this because I know from my own experience that you must look and see what is in or on the water, be very stealthy and conceal yourself as much as you possibly can, and fish as fine as possible and with small flies that suggest the food insects of the trout, particularly black patterns, and especially during the warm months. When the water is cold, you should fish deep and slow. When it is warm you should fish near the surface. Use flies that imitate the natural but also, so far as I am concerned, no one is ever going to take away my Woolly Worm and my wingless Butcher. They will be with me to the end.

THE WITCH OF BLAGDON

There is not a lovelier sight in England (pace Ramsbury and Hurstbourne Priors in buttercup time) than Blagdon from the Butcombe end at sundown, with the tiny town straggling up the steep hillside like a Bavarian village, the red roofs of the houses peeping out of the thick orchards (with never a Methodist chapel to shock the artist's eye), and the evening sunlight setting the windows of the old church aglow and flushing with purple pink the glassy surface of the lake.

There is a stillness here that belongs to no other valley. You can hear the 'plop' of the big trout far out half a mile away. You can talk to your friend across the water when the sun is down without ever raising your voice, and hear the scream of his reel in the blackness, and Blagdon is about seven miles round, and he may be half the length of the lake away from you.

But the dominant impression in my mind is the lovely colour of the evening light upon the valley as you face it looking east. It has a crimson velvet glow which hangs like an aura on the meadows and makes the shores and the scalloped hills burn with fires. It is Devonshire clay here and the whole landscape warms pink and deepens to purple-black as the sun goes down.

I know, too, that there was once a witch in the valley and that they drowned her when they let the water in; and one night as I grope my way home in the dark I shall stumble on Hänsel and Gretel asleep on the grass in a mist of white angels, with the myriad million stars of the Milky Way and the golden lights of Blagdon shining on their heads and winking in the watery glass at their feet.

HARRY PLUNKET GREENE, *Where the Bright Waters Meet,* 1924.

CONRAD VOSS BARK

*

As Time Went By

IT IS an interesting alleyway of history that the first description of dry fly fishing came in a book written by a Devon angler, G.P.R. Pulman, in 1841. There has been a deal of speculation about Pulman, especially how he came to know about fishing the dry fly, and even more especially from those who think the dry fly method evolved on the chalk streams of Hampshire.

Whether Pulman was the first to think of fishing the dry fly is unlikely. He makes no such claim. Moreover, he was well known to all the local anglers at Axminster, where he had a fishing tackle, stationery and newsagent's shop, with branches at Dorchester and Totnes, so that if the method had been new he would almost certainly have said so. He did not.

There is no doubt, however, about one thing. Pulman was the first to describe dry fly fishing with such clarity and perfection that all descriptions since then have been variations on his theme. Here is the passage from his book, from the first edition of 1841:

It is well known that trout feed much upon flies Ephemeridae—that is to say, the duns, etc; the habit of which insects is to sit upon the water; thus differing from the Phryganidae, which chiefly hover above it. When the state of the atmosphere is favourable for the production of this species, they come down in swarms, and the fish, in order to seize them the more easily, station themselves close under the surface, gently lifting their noses to catch them as they sail by. Now, as it is not the nature of things that this soaked artificial fly can swim upon the surface as the natural ones do, it follows the alternative and sinks below the rising fish, the notice of which it entirely escapes as they are looking upwards for the materials of their meal.

Let a dry fly be substituted for a wet one, the line switched a few times through the air to throw off the superabundant moisture, a judicious cast made just above the rising fish and the fly allowed to float towards and over them, and the chances are ten to one it will be taken as readily as the living insect.

We admit, however, to secure this, imitation of the predominant species is required; opining that if the fly be widely different in these respects the fish will be surprised and startled at the novelty presented and suspend feeding until the appearance of its known and familiar prey.

It is so clear and precise we want to know more. But that is all. The problems that remain are minor ones. Did Pulman use one fly or two? Two was the more usual number. And why in an earlier passage does he write about attaching his flies to the cast with a slip knot instead of the more usual loop which would normally mean that it would be far more difficult to change the fly? But these, as I say, are minor problems. There is no doubt that he deserves the title, bestowed on him some eighty years later, as 'the father of the dry fly'.

Little more is known about him. His favourite river was the Axe, at Slimlakes Bridge, just above Axminster, and he probably fished there from shortly after the Napoleonic wars until his retirement to Crewkerne in 1848. He knew something of ecology, had read Ronalds, and wrote rustic poems in the east Devon dialect. One of them expressed a sad farewell to his beloved River Axe:

> *An' my last wish shall be wi' my last vleeting breath—*
> *Lay my buones 'pon the bank that they dear waters lave,*
> *Mong th' turf let th' daisies and gulticups wave,*
> *An' thy murmurs be requiems over my grave!*

The rods that Pulman and his customers used would be between 10 and 13 feet long, in three ferruled sections, made of hickory, lancewood and bamboo, with a spare bamboo top carried in the hollow butt, and a spear at the end of the butt so that the rod could be placed upright on the ground instead of lying flat or being rested against a tree.

Pulman painted his rod matt black to avoid flash. Reels were brass, the lines of braided silk and horsehair, and the flies, tied to gut, would be looped on to a tapered gut 'collar' or cast, mostly two flies, one at the point (a 'stretcher') and one further up the cast called a bob or a drop fly. The ordinary upstream method of fishing was for the stretcher to be slightly sunk and the drop fly to be fished on the surface.

The names of the flies commonly used are familiar: the March Brown, Sandfly, Grannom, Early Red, Hare's Flax, Hawthorn, Yellow Dun, Iron Blue, Mayfly, Red Spinner, Willow Fly.

It is as well to remember that fishing the fly took place only when there was a surface hatch or some movement of trout near the surface; otherwise Pulman and everyone else at that time fished the worm or whatever livebait they fancied, small frogs, caddis grubs, maggots, minnows, anything that came to hand. There were no rules about fishing the fly, no fly-only waters, no licences needed, no limits on the number of fish or the size of fish that could be taken, no restrictions at all. Trout were a valuable food supply, probably the only fresh fish available in most inland towns and villages, and one went out fishing to bring back as many fish as one could. They were sometimes sold, no doubt, but it is on record that doctors and schoolmasters and clergymen who went fishing used to distribute their catch to their friends and the poor and needy of the parish, so that, as one of them wrote, 'the whole village would smell of frying trout for days afterwards'.

Most people imagine that the small moorland-fed rivers of Exmoor and Dartmoor are generally fished wet fly downstream but the main records that have survived of Victorian fishermen suggest that fishing upstream was preferred whenever possible. Get behind the trout's tail, keep your head low, and throw the fly above him, is fairly typical advice that came from a South Molton surgeon, H.C. Cutcliffe, in 1863. He wrote a book on fly fishing in Devon while he was serving in India and one can appreciate his longing for home in passages of this kind:

Whilst I write, what thoughts flash back to my mind! How vividly do I picture the beautiful and homely English scenery on that type of small streams, the little Bray; bubbling merry little fellow—he always seems joyous and, by his music, so sweet to the fisherman's ear, what a welcome does he whisper to your very heart.

The Bray and the upper Mole he fished, and was obviously passionately in love with them, but there was no question of exact imitation of the natural insect on these fast waters, merely a fly that gave an impression of a living creature. They were hackled, not winged, and the colour of hackle and dubbing must match and complement each other. The hackles must be sharp and the best obtainable. He used three or four patterns of various colours and shades. He also had good advice about tackle and was the first, so far as I know, to suggest that anglers should always wear rubber waders reaching to the fork 'which are sold at Cordings of Temple Bar'.

Sometimes Cutcliffe fished his flies on the surface, sometimes just below the surface, where they would no doubt suggest 'the several larvae and pupae that are washed into the stream'. Like Pulman, when the trout were not in position to take the surface fly he fished the worm or bait, and one of his favourite baits was the cow-dung beetle, which he found convenient to carry in an empty half-pound gunpowder tin. He had two rods with him, one for fly, the other for bait, the second rod 'carried by a servant, who can be trusted, because this is always at hand and economises time considerably'.

The tackle of these early Victorians would impress us today as being awkward and cumbersome but there was no doubt they could use heavy rods with considerable delicacy and skill. 'You must learn', wrote Cutcliffe, 'to pick every fish out of his particular hole and not trust generally to any fish your flies are washed over'. The more one reads Cutcliffe and Pulman the more one realises how good they must have been.

Towards the end of the nineteenth century, by about 1890, the tourists began to arrive, much to the annoyance of most of the locals, who until then had had the rivers to themselves. Among the invaders was a London barrister, Claude F. Wade, who wrote a guidebook to the Exmoor streams which was published in 1903. Wade himself, a devout fisherman, was also annoyed by another kind of tourist who searched Watersmeet and Badgworthy Water on Exmoor for the places mentioned in R.D. Blackmore's best-selling novel *Lorna Doone*. Wade was very annoyed when, fishing the river Lyn, he was stopped by people who wanted to know where Lorna Doone's cottage was and where was Gurt Jan Ridd's waterfall? 'A lot of nonsense', grumbled Wade. But it was inevitable. The West Country had been opened by the railways to the world outside.

Wade fished the Lyn for about forty years, staying at Lynmouth, hiring a pony and trap to take him up to the moors. The trout were small but rose well to the dry fly and he was full of advice, about flies and tackle, as well as how to dress for the moors. 'I think a black bowler hat or a very old and dinghy white one is the best to wear, and not a cap, because you ought to be able to wind at least two collars round your headgear.' Anglers wearing bowler hats must have looked a little out of place to tourists searching for Carver Doone.

One problem that comes up time and again in reading Wade, Cutcliffe and Pulman is what they actually meant when they wrote, as they often did, about 'working' the fly. It took me a long time before I realised that they were describing what a later generation who had been brought up on Skues, Sawyer and Kite would call an induced take.

Working or drawing the fly is described very clearly in a rather rare paperback, published privately at Launceston, at some unknown date, but probably around 1913. The author, Charles Rabley, was a schoolmaster at Ashwater, in west Devon, who fished the Tamar, the Carey, Wolf and Thrushel from about 1883 for some forty years. He clearly was a dry fly fisherman, fishing his team of two flies upstream—and again you notice the prevalence of upstream fishing in the West Country—but one day something happened. It is best described in his own words.

When fishing the Carey on a lovely June day I was completely baffled in all my efforts for success with the fly rod, although many trout were sporting in a promising stickle. Having fished through it blank I sat down and watched the fun going on, and never remember seeing the fish leaping so high into the air.

I started again at the bottom of the same water, and allowing the flies to sink some little distance, drew them slowly from the opposite bank across the water towards and above me. After a few draws a tug was felt, and as the line was already straight I held on, hooked the first fish and landed it. Continuing, and without seeing my flies, I took seven trout averaging above ¼lb, in 'drawing' the water the second time. Not content with this novelty, after a short interval I tried again and got two more.

Since then, under the same sporting conditions, I have adopted
with success the same plan on many occasions and now feel
convinced that trout do feed freely below the surface on insects and
can be caught with the artificial fly by touch as well as by sight.

It was really quite extraordinary that fly fishermen of Rabley's
day were so convinced that fly fishing was a matter of surface
activity that they seemed really quite surprised when an artificial
fly was taken below the surface. Rabley had no idea why this
should be so. He was interested merely in the presentation of the
fly, not in the reasons for the take, and though he could quote
Wordsworth at will, and did so, his knowledge of entomology was
negligible. That did not make him the worse as a fisherman. Many
times, he wrote, he would come back with over a hundred trout in
his basket and spend a large part of the next day distributing them
round the village.

Rabley's flies included the March Brown and the Hare's Fleck,
and the two patterns which are generally accepted as having been
first tied in the West Country—the Blue Upright and the Pheasant
Tail. The west has had many good fly dressers and still has for that
matter. There was R.S. Austin of Tiverton, whose Red Spinner is
better known as Tup's Indispensible, and more recently Peter
Deane, whose Beacon Beige, a splendid general pattern to represent the olive dun, was developed from the Beige Fly, first tied by
a member of the Wills family, at Dulverton, in Somerset, when he
was home on leave from the Somme in 1917.

Now for salmon and sea trout fishing—but here there is a
remarkable gap. Cutcliffe, Pulman, Rabley—none of them mention salmon and sea trout at all. It is as though the fish simply
didn't exist. The reason is, of course, that for the average trout
fisherman they didn't. There was little or no salmon fishing
available.

Most of the salmon—and one presumes also the sea trout—that
ran West Country rivers were taken by extensive daily and even
nightly netting by the staff for the owners of the big estates, the
landed and aristocratic families that owned many miles of the
rivers and the estuaries. The netting rights were strictly preserved,
not only in the estuaries but in the rivers themselves. Salmon were
a commercial asset, to be harvested in the most economical way,
like any other natural resource. The idea of catching salmon, by

rod and line, for pleasure as well as for eating, was slow to penetrate.

A contemporary account of fly fishing for salmon on one of the big ducal estates just before the First World War gives something of the atmosphere of the time. The duke would never fish until the head ghillie had assured him there were plenty of salmon in the pools and that they were in a taking mood. If the ghillie had caught several fish himself that morning the duke would get into his Rolls-Royce and be driven down to the bank. The chauffeur and the footman laid out a picnic. A little later the duchess and the children would come to watch. The estate workers were forbidden to be anywhere near, except for the chauffeur, the ghillie, and the footman.

There was little change in what must have been an idyllic, or at least a privileged, existence, until after the 1939–45 war. Then, many of the big estates, suffering from ever-increasing taxation, began to be broken up. Fishing rights were gradually acquired by syndicates and hotels and clubs. More and more good salmon fishing became available to the public in a considerable period of social change that seems likely to increase even faster as time goes by.

Th' Plizures o' th' Angle

An' I shall write, an 'zing, an' tull,
Th' plizures o' th' angle;
An' do et all to pleyze myzull
An' not wi' others wrangle.

A happy life ez passed by we
Who in th' fiels da like to be,
An' by th' stream ta strake about
Wi' rod an' line, a-ketchin trout.

Poem in the east Devon dialect
by G.P.R. PULMAN, of Axminster, 1853.

Where to Fish

Where to Fish

THE WEST COUNTRY has probably the largest number of game fishing rivers of any region of England. In the three counties of Somerset, Devon and Cornwall, there are over sixty rivers and streams running down from the uplands of Dartmoor, Exmoor and Bodmin. Some offer excellent salmon fishing, most have a good mid-summer run of sea trout, and all of them hold an abundance of wild brown trout. The major salmon river is the Tamar, followed by the Taw, Torridge, Exe, Fowey, Camel, Tavy, Dart, Teign and Lyn. There are also some thirty reservoirs and lakes with first class rainbow and brown trout fishing.

Nearly all these rivers and lakes have fishing available for the visiting fly fisherman and set out below are the main trout-stocked reservoirs and lakes, the major fishing hotels, and the largest fishing clubs, associations and private owners who have water for visitors. Addresses of clubs are not included as secretaries change, but these addresses are obtainable from the fisheries department of the regional water authorities.

In addition to obtaining permission to fish from the fishery owner, it is a legal requirement to hold a current regional water authority rod licence. This can be obtained from the water authority or their agents—mainly fishing hotels, post offices and tackle shops. Reservoir permits normally include the cost of the licence.

WATER AUTHORITY ADDRESSES

BRISTOL WATERWORKS COMPANY   Woodford Lodge, Chew Stoke, Bristol BS18 8XH Tel: Chew Magna (0272) 332339

WESSEX WATER AUTHORITY   PO Box 9, King Square, Bridgwater TA6 3EA Tel: Bridgwater (0278) 457333

SOUTH WEST WATER AUTHORITY   Peninsula House, Rydon Lane, Exeter, EX2 7HR Tel: Exeter (0392) 219666

FISHING HOTELS

Somerset

CARNARVON ARMS HOTEL   Dulverton, Somerset Tel: Dulverton (0398) 23302
Rivers Exe and Barle (salmon and brown trout), Haddeo (brown trout), 5½ miles private fishing, individual beats. Tackle for sale or hire.

EXMOOR FOREST HOTEL   Simonsbath, Via Minehead, Somerset Tel: Exford (064383) 341
Rivers Barle and Bray (brown trout), 9 miles private fishing. Own boat on Wimbleball reservoir.

TARR STEPS HOTEL   Hawkridge, Dulverton, Somerset Tel: Winsford (064 385) 293
River Barle (brown trout), 3½ miles private fishing. Flies for sale.

Devon

ARUNDELL ARMS HOTEL   Lifton, Devon Tel: Lifton (0566) 84666
Rivers Tamar and Lyd (salmon, sea trout and brown trout), Thrushel (sea trout and brown trout), Carey and Wolf (brown trout), 20 miles private fishing, individual beats. 2½ acre stocked trout lake. Two full-time bailiffs and instructors, tuition and courses. Tackle for sale or hire.

DEER PARK HOTEL   Honiton, Devon Tel: Honiton (0404) 2064
River Otter (brown trout), 5 miles private fishing. Bailiff and tuition. Tackle for hire.

ENDSLEIGH HOUSE   Milton Abbot, Nr Tavistock, Devon Tel: Milton Abbot (082 287) 248
River Tamar (salmon), 9 miles private fishing. Two small trout lakes. Full-time bailiff. Flies for sale.

FOREST INN   Hexworthy, Nr Princetown, Yelverton, Devon Tel: Poundsgate (03643) 211
No private fishing, but centrally situated for the Duchy of Cornwall fishing (brown trout and sea trout) on 40 miles of the Dart and tributaries.

FOX AND HOUNDS HOTEL   Eggesford, Chulmleigh, north Devon
Tel: Chulmleigh (0769) 80345
Rivers Taw and Little Dart (salmon, sea trout, brown trout),
3 miles private fishing.

HALF MOON INN   Sheepwash, Beaworthy, Devon Tel: Black
Torrington (040 923) 376
Rivers Middle Torridge (salmon, sea trout, brown trout), Upper
Torridge (brown trout), 6 miles private fishing, individual beats.
Advice and tuition. Tackle for sale or hire.

RISING SUN INN   Umberleigh, north Devon Tel: High Bickington
(0769) 60447
River Taw (salmon, sea trout, brown trout), 3½ miles private
fishing, individual beats. Tackle for sale.

RIVER ASSOCIATIONS, CLUBS AND PRIVATE FISHERIES

These are the main sources of river fishing available to visitors on
day or weekly permits. In addition, many of the fishing hotels
issue permits to non-residents when their beats are not allocated to
hotel guests. Addresses of the clubs and associations are not
included as the secretaries change, often yearly, but these are
obtainable from the fisheries department of the South West Water
Authority (SWWA).

DEVON

Avon
South Brent and Aveton Gifford 14½ miles Avon. Brown trout, sea
trout, occasional salmon. Permits from Avon Fishing Association,
post offices at Loddiswell and Diptford, and tackle shops at Totnes
and Kingsbridge. Weekly and seasonal tickets only.

Shipley Bridge to Avon Dam 1½ miles Avon. Brown trout. Free to
anglers holding SWWA licence.

Dart

Dartmoor 40 miles on West and East Dart, Cherry Brook, Walla Brook, Swincombe Brook, Blackbrook. Brown trout, sea trout, occasional salmon. Permits from Duchy of Cornwall, Bowhill, Brandninch, Exeter EX5 4LH. Tel: Hele (039 288) 210. Also from Forest Inn at Hexworthy, Arundell Arms at Lifton, and post offices at Princetown and Postbridge.

Buckfastleigh to Totnes Weir 5/6 miles Dart. Brown trout, sea trout, occasional salmon. Permits from Dart Angling Association and local tackle shops.

Exe

Exeter 3 miles Exe and Creedy. Salmon. Permits from SWWA.

Hemyock 4 miles Exe and Culm. Brown trout. Permits from Upper Culm Fishing Club.

Lyn East

Lynmouth 6 miles Glenthorne and Watersmeet Fisheries. Salmon, sea trout, brown trout. Permits from SWWA.

Tavy and Plym

Yelverton 10 miles Tavy, Walkham, Plym and Meavy. Salmon, sea trout, brown trout. Permits from Tavy, Walkham and Plym Fishing Club, and tackle shops at Tavistock, Yelverton and Plymouth.

Teign

Newton Abbot 18 miles Teign and Bovey. Salmon, sea trout, brown trout. Permits from Lower Teign Fishing Association and local tackle shops.

Steps Bridge to Chagford Bridge 12 miles Teign. Salmon, sea trout, brown trout. Permits from Upper Teign Fishing Association or from the Angler's Rest, Fingle Bridge, Drewsteignton and local tackle shops.

Torridge

Torrington, Beaford and Hatherleigh 8 miles Torridge, Bray, Taw and Yeo. Salmon, sea trout, brown trout. Permits from Mr J. Gawesworth, Caynton House, Mill Street, Torrington, North Devon. Tel: Torrington (0805) 23256.

Beaford 1½ miles Torridge. Salmon, sea trout, brown trout. Permits from Group Captain P. Norton-Smith, Little Warham, Beaford, Winkleigh, north Devon. Tel: Beaford (080 53) 317.

Torrington 5 miles Torridge. Salmon, sea trout, brown trout, permits from Mr C.R. Rowe (Lower Torridge Fishery), Oak Tree Cottage, Stafford Way, Dolton, Winkleigh, north Devon. Tel: Dolton (080 54) 389.

Holsworthy 7 miles Upper Torridge, brown trout; 2 miles Lower Torridge, salmon and sea trout. Permits from Woodford Bridge Hotel, Milton Damerel, Nr Holsworthy, north Devon. Tel: Milton Damerel (040 926) 481.

CORNWALL
Camel and Fowey

Wadebridge 5½ miles Camel and Allen (part tidal). Salmon, sea trout, brown trout. Permits from Wadebridge and District Angling Association. No visitors' permits in December.

Bodmin 11 miles Camel and Fowey. Salmon, sea trout, brown trout. Permits from Bodmin Anglers Association.

Liskeard 30 miles Camel, Fowey, Seaton, Lynher, Inny, East and West Looe. Salmon, sea trout, brown trout. Permits from Liskeard and District Angling Club, local tackle shops and Rilla Mill post office. No visitors' permits after 15 October.

Lanhydrock 2 miles Fowey. Salmon and sea trout. Permits from Lanhydrock Angling Association, c/o The National Trust, The Estate Office, Lanhydrock Park, Bodmin, Cornwall. Tel: Bodmin (0208) 4281. No visitors' day tickets after 30 September.

Tamar

Kilkhampton 6 miles Upper Tamar and Claw. Brown trout. Permits from Bude Angling Association, and Bude and Holsworthy tackle shops.

Launceston 8/9 miles Tamar, Inny, Carey, Kensey, Ottery. Salmon, sea trout, brown trout. Permits from Launceston Anglers Association and Launceston tackle shops.

RESERVOIR TROUT FISHING

Information on seasons and stocking can be obtained from the fisheries department of the relevant water authority. Self-service permits for bank and boat fishing are generally available at the reservoirs.

Avon (Somerset)   Bristol Waterworks
The Barrows (26, 39 and 60 acres). Barrow Gurney, off A38 about 5 miles south of Bristol.
Blagdon Lake (440 acres). Off A368, near junction with A38 near Bristol.
Chew Valley Lake (1200 acres). Off A368, near junction with A38 near Bristol.

Somerset   Wessex Water
Clatworthy (130 acres). Near Wiveliscombe.
Durleigh (80 acres). Near Bridgwater.
Hawkridge (32 acres). Near Bridgwater.
Sutton Bingham (142 acres). Near Yeovil.

Somerset   South West Water
Wimbleball (374 acres). Near Brompton Regis, Dulverton.

Devon   South West Water
Burrator (150 acres). Near Yelverton, Plymouth, off B3212.
Fernworthy (76 acres). Near Chagford.
Kennick and Tottiford (45 and 35 acres). Near Bovey Tracey.
Wistlandpound (41 acres). Off B3226 near Bratton Flemming, Barnstaple.

Cornwall   South West Water
Argal (65 acres). Near Penryn, Falmouth, off B3291.
Porth (40 acres). Near Newquay, off A3059.
Siblyback (140 acres). Near Upton Cross, Liskeard off, B3254.
Upper Tamar Lake (81 acres). Near Kilkhampton, Bude, off B3254 and A39.

PRIVATE LAKE FISHING

Devon

Stafford Moor (22 acres). Off B3220 Exeter to Bideford road between Winkleigh and Beaford. Day tickets from Mr Andrew Joynson, Dolton, Winkleigh, North Devon. Tel: Dolton (080 54) 360.

SALMON AND SEA TROUT
AVERAGE ROD CATCHES 1971–80

	Salmon	Sea trout
AVON and ERME	10	197
CAMEL	280	996
DART and tributaries	133	380
EXE and tributaries	257	16
FOWEY	302	1205
LYN	163	75
LYNHER	126	296
PLYM	49	246
TAMAR and tributaries	712	476
TAVY and tributaries	97	673
TAW and tributaries	348	1190
TEIGN	71	819
TORRIDGE and tributaries	183	709

Note: These figures are supplied by the South West Water Authority from licence returns made by the rods fishing the rivers. They are only an indication of catch since many rods omit to make a return. The true figures are likely to be far higher.

BIBLIOGRAPHY

Anthony Bridges, *Modern Salmon Fishing*, 1939.

Brian Clarke, *The Pursuit of Stillwater Trout*, 1975.

Brian Clarke and John Goddard, *The Trout and the Fly*, 1980.

H. C. Cutcliffe, FRCS, *The Art of Trout Fishing in Rapid Streams*, 1863.

Kenneth Dawson, *Salmon and Trout in Moorland Streams*, 1928.

Joan and Terry Doyle, *Tamar Valley Traveller*, Cornish Safari Co., 1978.

Hugh Falkus, *Sea Trout Fishing* (2nd edn), Witherby 1975.

Negley Farson, *Going Fishing*, 1942 (2nd edn 1981, Clive Holloway Books).

Sarah Foot, *Following the River Fowey*, Bossiney Books, 1979, *Following the Tamar*, Bossiney Books, 1980.

E. Garrow Green, *Trout Fishing in Brooks*, 1920.

John Goddard, *Trout Fly Recognition*, 1966.

L. R. N. Gray, *Torridge Fishery*, 1957.

Edward Grey, *Fly Fishing* (1920 edn), 1899.

F. M. Halford, *The Dry Fly Man's Handbook*, 1913.

J. Heddon, *A Brief History of the Floating Fly*, Fly Dressers Guild, 1980.

J. Waller Hills, *A History of Fly Fishing for Trout*, 1920.

Lord Home, *Border Reflections*, Collins, 1979.

W. H. Lawrie, *A Reference Book of English Trout Flies*, 1967.

T. C. Kingsmill Moore, *A Man May Fish*, 1967.

Donald Overfield, *Famous Flies and their Originators*, 1972.

G. P. R. Pulman, *Vade Mecum of Fly Fishing for Trout*, edns 1841, 1846 and 1851. *Rustic Sketches*, 1853.

Harry Plunket Greene, *Where the Bright Waters Meet*, 1924, the Witherby edn, 1969.

Chas A. Rabley, *Devonshire Trout Fishing*, 1913.

Alfred Ronalds, *A Fly Fisher's Entomology*, 1836.

G. W. Soltau, *Trout Flies of Devon and Cornwall*, 1847.

George Scotcher, *A Fly Fisher's Legacy*, 1810. Honeydun Press edn, 1974.

Claude F. Wade, *Exmoor Streams*, 1903.

C. F. Walker, *Lake Flies and their Imitation*, Herbert Jenkins, 1960.

Leonard West, *The Natural Trout Fly and its Imitation*, 2nd edn, 1921.

Izaac Walton and Charles Cotton, *The Compleat Angler*, 1676, Folio Society edn, 1962.

A. Courtney Williams, *A Dictionary of Trout Flies*, 1949 (1965 edn).

Henry Williamson, *Salar the Salmon*, Faber edn 1972. *A Clear Water Stream*, 1958.

Dermot Wilson, *Fishing the Dry Fly*, A&C Black 1957.

INDEX

Adams, Horace 14, 15
Arundell Arms 14
Austin, R. S. 118
Avon 59, 68, 85
Avon Dam 107
Axe 8, 9, 114

Barle 1, 59, 89
Bedford, Dukes of 15, 22
Bell, Dr H. A. 104
Blackbrook 59, 67
Blagdon 1, 104–106
  witch of 112
Bodmin Moor 101, 108
Bray 38, 115, 116
Bridges, Antony 41
Bristol Waterworks 104
  see also Water Authority
    addresses
Buckingham, Roy 14, 17
Buckland, Frank 34
Burrator 107

Camel 8, 9, 54, 102–103
Carey 1, 73, 75, 76, 83, 117
Carnarvon Arms 20
Cherry Brook 60, 85
Chew 1–4, 104–106
Clatworthy 106
Clubs, fishing 124–126
Cordings 116
Courtney Williams 64
Cutcliffe, H. C. 115, 116

Dalch 38
Dart 8, 25, 41, 44, 47, 59–61,
  67–69, 82
Dartmoor 4, 25, 32, 39, 42, 65, 67,
  73, 85, 107
Dawson, Kenneth 14, 58, 63
Deane, Peter 118
Duchy of Cornwall 59

Endsleigh 14, 15
Erme 54
Exe 1, 8, 9, 19–21, 42, 47, 59, 62,
  83, 85
Exmoor 19, 21, 32, 59, 65, 106

Falkus, Hugh 36, 53
Farson, Negley 70, 100
Fernworthy 107
The Field 104
Fishing club addresses 124–126
Fishing hotel addresses 123, 124
Flyfishers' Club 84, 104
Fortescue Arms 31
Fowey 8, 9, 54, 101–103
Fox and Hounds 32

Glenthorne Fishery 67
Gray, see Lemon Gray
Greene, H. Plunket 112
Grey, Earl 24, 69

Half Moon Inn 28, 32
Hardy Corfe, R. C. 104
Home, Lord 70
Hotel addresses 123–124

Ivens, T. C. 110

Jones, John 108

Kennick 107
Kingsmill Moore, T. C. 57, 100

Lake fishing addresses 127–128
Lemon Gray 34
Lyd 4, 49, 53, 73, 74, 83
Lyn 8, 59, 61, 67, 116, 117
Lynher 8, 9, 53

Marsden, Lionel 22
Marshall, Howard 19

Melbourne, Lord 24
Meldon 29, 107
Mole, 31, 32, 38, 116

Netboy, Anthony 26
Netting, effects of 37, 39
Nicholson, Lance 20
Norton Smith, Group Captain 30

Okement 25, 38
Otter 85, 86, 88

Peal, see Sea trout
Pierce, Tom 31
Plym 59
Porth 107
Pulman, G. P. R. 113–115, 120

Rabley, Charles 117–118
Rainfall 4, 8, 31
Reservoir trout fishing addresses
    127
Rising Sun 32
Rivers, ecology of 8–10
Russell, Lord Hugh 22

Salmon
    Big fish 22, 30, 31, 32
    Catches (1971–80) 128
    Flies 14–16, 20–22, 30, 34, 43, 44
    Genetic influences 10
    Weirs, problem of 23, 37, 38
    and see also separate chapters on
        salmon rivers
Sea trout
    Catches (1971–80) 128
    Fishing methods 44–46, 47–56
    Flies 34–36, 49, 52, 55, 102
    Links with brown trout 10
    and see also separate chapters on
        salmon and sea trout rivers
Siblyback 108
Soltau, G. W. 23

South West Water Authority 33,
    38, 39, 67
Spate rivers 8
    flash floods 8, 36
    spring spate 40
Stafford Moor 108–110
Sutton Bingham 106
Symons, Herbie 15, 16

Tamar 1, 8, 13–19, 42, 53, 71, 72,
    85, 117
Tamara, legend of 12
Tavy 25, 42, 44, 53, 59
Taw, 1, 8, 9, 25–29, 53, 85
Teign 8, 25, 42, 44, 59, 61, 66, 85
Thrushel 117
Tiddy 47
Torridge 1, 8, 25–39, 53, 85
Trout of the moors 58–69
    of the valleys 79–83
    dry fly tactics 58–69, 79–83
    wet fly tactics 90–103
Trout flies 62–65, 68, 69, 77, 89,
    91, 92, 95, 97, 99, 118

Upper Tamar Lake 107, 108

Victorian fishermen 115, 116

Wade, Claude F. 100, 116
Walker, C. F. 107
Water Authority addresses 122,
    123
Watersmeet 67, 116
Where to fish guide 122–128
White, M. R. L. 104
Williamson, Henry 25, 26, 40
Wills family 118
Wimbleball 106
Wistlandpound 108
Wolf 117

Yeo 38

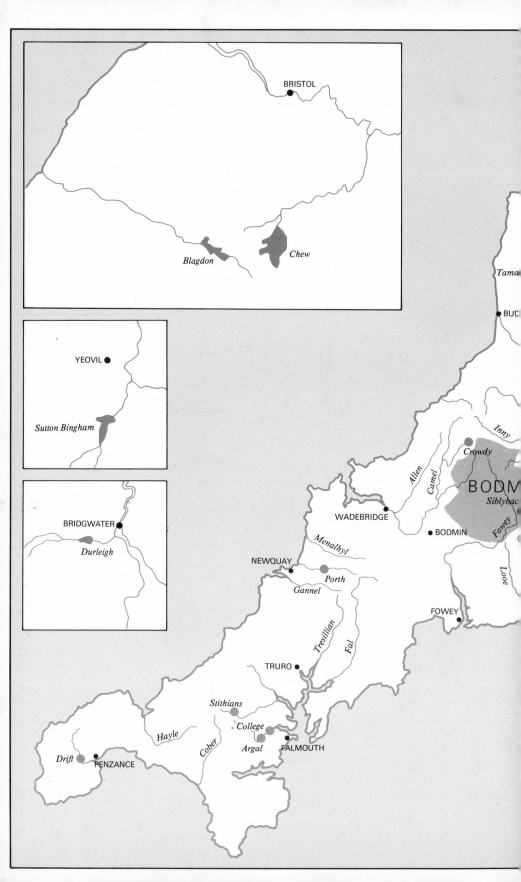